STOICISM
AND
ST. FRANCIS DE SALES

STOICISM
AND
ST. FRANCIS DE SALES

William C. Marceau

Toronto Studies in Theology
Volume 44

The Edwin Mellen Press
Lewiston/Queenston/Lampeter

Library of Congress Cataloging-in-Publication Data

Marceau, William.
    Stoicism and St. Francis de Sales / William C. Marceau.
       p.   cm. -- (Toronto studies in theology ; v. 44)
    Includes bibliographical references.
    ISBN   0-88946-749-8
    1. Francis, de Sales, Saint, 1567-1622. 2. Stoics--Study and
teaching--France--History--17th century. 3. Epictetus--Influence.
4. Seneca, Lucius Annaeus, ca. 55 B.C.-ca. 39 A.D.--Influence.
I. Title. II. Title: Stoicism and Saint Francis de Sales.
III. Series.
BX4700.F85M25513   1989
282'.09--dc20
                                         89-29988
                                             CIP

This is volume 44 in the continuing series
Toronto Studies in Theology
Volume 44 ISBN 0-88946-749-8
TST Series ISBN 0-88946-975-X

A CIP catalog record for this book
is available from the British Library.

The Edwin Mellen Press
Box 450
Lewiston, New York
USA 14092

The Edwin Mellen Press
Box 67
Queenston, Ontario
CANADA, L0S 1L0

The Edwin Mellen Press, Ltd.
Lampeter, Dyfed, Wales
UNITED KINGDOM SA48 7DY

Printed in the United States of America

To
Mother and Dad

NIHIL OBSTAT
Reverend John P. Connolly, OSFS
Censor Deputatus

IMPRIMATUR
Patrick Cardinal O'Boyle
Apostolic Administrator
of the Archdiocese of Washington

May 3, 1973

Contents

Author's Notes

I should like to express my gratitude to the Institute of Salesian Studies, and particularly to Father William Gallagher, O.S.F.S. He has aided and encouraged me in my efforts to know better St. Francis de Sales.

Translation is always difficult. It is even more so of one's own work. This volume is no exception. For their corrections and suggestions of the translation, I am indebted to Father Leo Hetzler, C.S.B. and Dr. Florence Weinberg. To Mrs. R. Kalb I offer my gratitude for her patient cooperation.

References throughout the English translation are complete as in the original French edition. However, when necessary and/or possible, the English sources are placed in parentheses after the original reference.

Key to English references used to Salesian works:

Ryan	Ryan, John, *Introduction to the Devout Life*, New York, Image Books, 1950, 314 pp.
Ryan, I	Ryan, John, *On the Love of God by Saint Francis de Sales*, New York, Image Books, 1963, Books I-VI.
Ryan, II	*Ibid.*, Books VII-XII.
Gasquet	Gasquet and Mackey, *The Spiritual Conferences of Saint Francis de Sales*, Westminster, Md., Newman Press, 1962, 406 pp.
Stopp	Stopp, Elisabeth, *St. Francis de Sales – Selected Letters*, New York, Harper and Brothers, 1960, 318 pp.

All references to the *Works* of St. Francis de Sales in French are to the Annecy Edition. The following reference system has been adopted: tome number and page or pages. The English source appears in parentheses when possible.

Foreword

William J. Gallagher, O.S.F.S.

In the history and development of Christian spirituality, St. Francis de Sales stands among the distinguished. His reflection upon the Christian mystery coupled with the knowledge culled from his ministry resulted in both a holy life and an instruction of value for many – an instruction that trancends the age in which he lived and worked. The transcendence did not cause him to be irrelevant, for, indeed, he spoke meaningfully to the people whom he directed. He was a man of his time, versed in, but not overwhelmed by, the currents of thought and the turmoil of change of the late sixteenth and early seventeenth centuries.

He possessed the gift of being able to distill the intellectual streams that swirled about him and develop a practical synthesis of Christian living. William C. Marceau, C.S.B., in this work delves into his relationship with the Neo-Stoicism of the period. The result is an excellent presentation of some of the most essential elements of Salesian spirituality.

In a world confused and confounded by materialism, Francis de Sales remains a source of conversion to life according to the revelation of God. Moreover, he presents the Christian with the invaluable example of converting and purifying trends found in society for the benefit and growth of the people of God.

INTRODUCTION

Stoicism is unquestionably among the great systems of thought which has interested the world. Zeno, who founded it, is one of the patriarchs of philosophy, and his views, developed by his successors, share with those of Pythagorus, Plato and Aristotle that unique honor of having excited minds. Unlike Aristotle and Plato, however, Zeno gave to metaphysical speculation a role of only secondary importance. Like Pythagorus, he was interested in the moral direction of humanity. Noble minds, illustrious writers, distinguished philosophers, eminent jurists, celebrated men of state and even emperors became glorious marching under Stoicism's banner. During recurring periods of decadence and of moral decrepitude, they had sought in these doctrines the principle of regeneration of society: and if this regeneration had been possible through a purely human system, Stoicism would perhaps have brought it about. But other things proved necessary in order to resurrect the cadaver and to make new blood run in its veins. Stoicism had the glory of undertaking the effort, but Christianity brought it to its completion. To have been the latter's rival and opponent in such difficult struggles was a great honor for Stoicism. When there existed only this regeneration to be achieved, it would have been sufficient simply to prick the curiosity of the philosopher and to provoke on his part a comparative study of the two systems. But the two philosophies have other similarities. Considerable parts of their moral doctrine are as medals struck with the same image. The fathers themselves recognized this. Their *Seneca noster* is known by everyone. Saint Jerome, for example, in his commentary on Isaiah recalls this agreement.[1] We know that Saint Charles Borromeo read Epictetus and that Saint Niles had put him in the hands of his religious, though with some slight changes. Finally, and especially, scholars are very aware that Saint Francis de Sales read Epictetus as well as other Stoics during his years at Clermont and even in later years. Thus he praises Epictetus writing: "I marvel at that poor, good man, Epictetus."[2] But can we say simply that Saint Francis was Stoic and that he taught a doctrine which was, in a sense, a Christianized Stoicism? It is important to show that, in spite of the similarities that Stoicism and Christianity's Salesian doctrine do share, the two theories are far from being identical. Indeed, it is a gross illusion to imagine that the philosophical doctrines of Zeno could advantageously replace the philosophical and religious doctrine of Solomon.[3] We undertake this task in order to determine if there is true Stoicism in the works of Saint Francis de Sales. We shall seek a clear idea of these two teachings in order to examine them successively in their relationships, their differences and, finally, the respective influences that they exercised on the works of Saint Francis de Sales.

We know from the works of Strowski, of Zanta, and of Busson that the humanistic Renaissance introduced into France a tendency for Stoic doctrine. Its influence, at the end of the sixteenth century especially, is indisputable, not only in regard to the theoretical thought and literary forms but also to practical attitudes. Indeed, Stoicism persisted in a very lively way for a century. Thus Malebranche considered it timely to criticize "the most honorable sect of philosophers...whom many people glorify by embracing their sentiments."[4] These sentiments Malebranche judged incompatible with the Gospel. But this incompatibility did not appear clear to everyone. Du Vair, for example, statesman and later churchman in those very troubled times, drew his moral certitudes and his courage as much from the Book of Nature composed by Seneca and Epictetus as from Holy Scripture, "the oracle of truth."

Introduction Endnotes

1   *Stoici nostro dogmati in plerisque concordant.*

2   *Oeuvres*, IV, p. 81 [Ryan, I, p. 96].

3   Justus Lipsius, *Introduction to Stoic Philosophy*.... 1, 17.

4   Malebranche, *Recherche de la Vérité*, V, 2.

CHAPTER I

Neo-Stoicism in the Seventeenth Century

Did Francis de Sales anticipate more contemporary adversaries or did he very loosely ally himself with a group of Neo-Stoics? To answer this question justly and truthfully, it is perhaps important to specify the characteristics of Stoicism in relation to his thought and position.

We are going to study three important Stoics in order to see if Saint Francis could have believed in Stoicism and in order to bring out an essential point – that there is no one Stoicism. There are only Stoics. After having evoked the old Stoicism, we shall discover how Stoicism was renewed in seventeenth-century France because of the humanist movement. Neo-Stoicism will become apparent through our glimpse of Christian humanism.[1] This Neo-Stoicism appears during the life of Francis de Sales (1567-1622).

The historian of Stoicism finds himself in the presence of two serious difficulties. The first is the duration of the evolution of Stoicism and the diversity of the phases through which the doctrine passed. Second is the state of his sources.

Numenius, a Neo-Platonic philosopher who lived in the second half of the eleventh century A. D., said of the Stoics, according to Eusebius: "The Stoics are in disagreement among themselves; these disagreements start at the outset of the school, and they have not yet ceased today."[2]

This statement is perfectly just; there never was an orthodox Stoic school. There is not a Stoicism; there are only Stoics. Chrysippus, according to Diogenes Laertius, differed on a very great number of points from his two predecessors, Zeno and Cleanthes. One could, as the saying goes, write a book on the differences. Subsequently, the differences were still more serious. But the historian must grasp these interior transformations and especially their value. It is possible to determine the general pattern. Historians habitually distinguish three major periods: old Stoicism with Zeno, Cleanthes and Chrysippus (end of the fourth century, third century B.C.); middle Stoicism, whose best-known representatives are Posidonius and Panetius, in the first century B.C.; and finally the new Stoicism which, under the Roman empire, counted among its masters Seneca, Epictetus and later Marcus Aurelius. It will be necessary to see what Stoicism was among its initial representatives and then in Epictetus, who is most important for us because of the readings of Saint Francis de Sales.

Like most ancient philosophers, Zeno assembled all the philosophical sciences under logic, physics, and ethics. However, here we shall limit ourselves to ethics because of our subject and the brevity of our work. Zeno defends a cosmological view and a materialistic and pantheistic theodicy. According to Zeno, in effect, all which exists is corporeal. That which is not corporeal is only abstraction, a creation of reason: hence no spirit is without matter, nor is matter without spirit. The world is composed of two principles: one passive and formless matter; the other active and divine, an ever-acting intelligence, the eternal reason of things, "a primitive and universal seed." And so it is that Zeno identifies what to the Christian would be the first efficient and extrinsic cause of the universe, namely God, with the formal and intrinsic causes. His God is not even that which is best in the universe, but He is the universe itself.

Now the same system of philosophy can have different nuances, according to the mind which continues it. Thus ancient Stoicism, which appears of a more strictly moral nature in Zeno, more intellectual and dialectic in Chrysippus, adopts with Cleanthes a particularly religious tone and a mystical aura. A few of the poems of Cleanthes, or fragments of the poems, have been conserved. One at least, in the form of a hymn to Zeus, is one of the most touching relics of ancient piety.

The hymn terminates in a prayer. It has invoked God by his true name. He becomes favorable due to praise magnifying his grandeur and recalling his good dispositions toward men. Finally, to conclude, the beseecher asks him to grant his needs. In this prayer of petition, the two beings actually form a relationship – God is all powerful, man has so many needs – and from these good divine dispositions, to which the faithful one has just given praise, the suppliant expects to derive benefit. By its religious sentiment as well as by its poetry, the hymn of Cleanthes prefigures the nightingale and the swan of the god of Epictetus.[3]

The impassioned preaching of the Stoic moral accounts for the originality and the greatness of Epictetus. The themes are few in number, but indefinitely repeated: absolute liberty of man who, even in irons or under torture, remains master of his actions; affirmation that good and evil depend on us, since they consist in properly directing these actions; indifference to exterior events; agreement of the wise man's will with destiny; identity of virtue and happiness; relationship of man with God. But, this preaching is never abstract nor monotonous. There is only wisdom which is lived and no other teaching than that of example. From this comes the constant recourse of Epictetus to the exaltation of a few individual "types": Ulysses, who symbolizes the Victories of the soul of the wise man over the assaults and temptations of the exterior world; Hercules, the active hero, the individual who has gained his independence through his actions and not through his knowledge.

In the history of philosophy, Epictetus himself particularly characterizes the Stoic moral: "the moral transfiguration of slavery,"[4] Nietzsche will say; but, inversely Pascal discerned in the *Discourses* some "principles of a diabolical pride":[5] if evil is only an opinion, if happiness depends on our will, man can bring about his own salvation, and hence his "misery" is denied.

God is at the center of Epictetus' preoccupations and his moral is profoundly inspired by his religious beliefs. The moral precepts are true divine precepts whose violation constitutes disobedience to God, and moral rectitude supposes a sane conception of the divinity:

> ...the first thing to learn is the following: there is a God and he exercises his Providence on the universe; man is incapable of hiding from him not only his actions, but even his intentions and his thoughts. Next, we must learn what these gods are. Because when one will have found them, one will try to become like them. In resembling them as much as possible, man will wish to please and to obey them.[6]

The ideal searched for is interior peace, deliverance "from sadness, fear, desire, envy, malevolence, avarice, effeminacy and intemperance. But it is not possible to eject these things otherwise than by looking to God only, by being consecrated to his commands."[7]

After having seen a few particular doctrines of these Stoics, it will be necessary to examine Stoicism from a triple point of view which embraces all the great questions of philosophy. Concentrating particularly on the moral part which is properly Stoic, our examination will touch upon the points of contact and the differences between the two doctrines relative to the principles and the rules they put into application.

According to Stoicism, man's and other being's good is the attainment of its end; its end is deduced from its nature; the nature of man is his reason. The body is only an accident and is not a part of his person. Man then must live in conformity with reason and constantly have a free, tranquil and strong soul. In order to be free, he must break himself loose from his passions and from the influence of exterior things, *abstine*, and as he is more certain to suppress his passions than to regulate them he must apply himself to the extirpating of his passions. In order to conserve his tranquility of soul he must accept steadfastly all the evils of life, *sustine*. And in order to accomplish both of these, he needs strength of soul. Whence the ataraxia or tranquility: from this serene region, he contemplates any earthly problems without being troubled by them: "Si fractus inlabatur orbis. Impavidum ferient ruinae."[8]

This is the state of the divinity, in which he participates already by the nature of his soul, and which is an emanation of it. From this point of view, he is equal to God. That is, he might even be considered superior to God because God is in this state by the privilege of his nature, and the wise man has conqered it by the strength of his will. Thus the wise man is perfect, and is aware of the cosmos. He is veritably a king, because he is master of his passions; he is rich, because all belongs to him alone who knows how to use everything. He is handsome, because the qualities of his mind are far above what his face reflects. He is invincible. He can fetter his body, but his soul will escape its bonds. He cannot fall from this state, and if suffering and pain become intolerable, he rids himself of it by voluntary death. Hence, remaining unshakeable in the unalterable calmness of his serene majesty, he passes tranquilly from life to death, and allows himself to pass into the state of nothingness. Or, by a pantheistic absorption, he is lost forever in the bosom of God.

Such is, in a few words, the Stoic doctrine.

In the sixteenth century, theology was in decline. It was comprised of an infinite division of questions which were far less than vital, its dry and cold syllogisms which could not nourish a heart avid for beauty and a barbaric Latin which was in direct contrast to that of the fathers. All this could only be repugnant to Christian humanists. Hence there is a return to antiquity, not in order to adopt it in its original spirit, but to try to orient it toward the faith and to reinvigorate it in evangelical sources. Then, among the ancient doctrines, along with Aristotle and Plato, Stoicism took a favored place. Undoubtedly, it had shown itself in its true light, denying the immortality of the soul, submitting everything to destiny and constructing its moral on the sole dignity of virtue to the exclusion of any Divinity.[9] But after the Ciceronian quarrel, humanist scholars turned their thoughts to Epictetus and Seneca; editions followed each other in accelerated rhythm; efforts were multiplied to learn the Neo-Stoic philosophers, and the attempts became so vigorous, so effective, that they were extended even to about 1660. Works only had to become adapted. Without doubt, they will lack the enthusiasm of the early fathers of the Church: writers no longer have any doctrine to establish and consequently to defend point by point against pagan philosophy; authors simply had to react in a moral and religious way, but, nevertheless, they turned their eyes toward these first defenders of the Church whose works were reedited. They learned from them how to win minds and hearts to good and to virtue in order to win them for God.

How did Saint Francis de Sales, a Christian writer, react to the confrontation of faith with Stoicism? He reacted according to the spirit of his time. As a Christian humanist during this period of Neo-Stoicism, he made the effort to close the gap which separated Christianity and Stoicism. At the same time, he safeguarded Orthodoxy. This does not mean that Saint Francis de Sales was Stoic, but rather that he was a true "child of his times."

A little like Epictetus, Saint Francis de Sales tried to communicate his faith to his disciples. But he did it by opening to everyone the sanctuary of the interior life and entering there by means of Catholic doctrine. There is nothing in him which aggravates learned men nor those who call themselves freethinkers; he senses that *the condition of the minds of 'his' century* demands that everything be founded on the solid rock of the dogmas of the faith. To touch upon the principal mysteries of his religion: the Trinity, the redemption, justification, the marvelous economy of grace; to expose the grandeurs of human origins and destinies, the means to adopt in order not to degenerate certain ones and to attain others; such is the goal that the author proposes to himself.

In order to fulfill this vast endeavor, he had to go back even to the pagan philosophies, not only in order to prove their emptiness and insufficiency, but still more to discover the notions of true worship and certain vestiges of truth to be found in several of the ancient philosophies. Far from scorning this "knowledge of the past which God earlier placed on the earth to serve as a steppingstone"[10] to knowing Him, he uses it to testify in favor of Catholic dogmas. A secret sympathy, a sort of affinity, draws the great soul of Saint Francis de Sales to the patriarchs of philosophy: Aristotle, Socrates, Plato, and Epictetus, "the best man of all antiquity." While he stigmatizes their errors, he often renders homage to their intellectual qualities, and even to their moral virtues; but he always is careful to point out the insufficiency of these purely natural virtues, and hence imperfect from the orthodox Christian point of view.

We certainly agree that the originality of Francis de Sales did not consist in proposing a precisely new doctrine. Should one advance such a contribution, it would be necessary to point out that the author of the *Introduction*, even when he is just beginning to write, says nothing that he has not learned from others – he acknowledges it openly – or that others have not said before him. His newness is not in this respect, but in the very particular choice that he wanted to make from among the teachings of his predecessors; in the principles which have directed, supported, animated his diligent synthesis; in the very personal tone of his work. Jean-Pierre Camus understood him very well. It was he who proposed to describe the "spirit" of Saint Francis de Sales; the spirit, and not the theories, the systems, as he would have done for Saint Augustine or Saint Thomas. And this spirit itself is not completely new either. How could it be, since it could only be one of the forms of the Christian spirit? If we pay attention to Richeome, we see that Francis de Sales' great merit is to have contributed his limpid, haunting, charming voice and to have imposed it on the world by the double authority of his genius and his own person.

It is the spirit of Christian humanism, of Sadolet or Reginald Pole, for example, but deliberately applied to the pious life and presented to all souls. Humanism in itself is neither Christian nor pagan: it can easily become one or the other, according to the characteristics of each humanist. Christian humanism does not teach in a didactic way but rather by implication the concern for the interior life and personal perfection. It was normally more speculative than practical. It counts saints among its adherents, but it is not in itself a school of sanctity. In any case, it seemed reserved, if not to the particularly intelligent, at least to an elite of well-born Catholics who had leisure, culture and the taste for ancient letters.[11] As such, it contained and developed a philosophy concerning general notions of God, man and the world. A philosophy, rather vague and uncertain from the very beginning, which had to fully agree finally with orthodox theology after arduous work of precision or correction. Thus have we seen Christian humanism, duly purified of every suspect element, triumphantly reign among the Fathers of Trent and mark with its noble impression a few of the most remarkable decisions. Philosophy, theology, learned disciplines to which the masses are not admitted, nevertheless have a real and deep influence on moral education and the sanctification of all men. Hence, after this slow evolution which had definitively united the best humanism with elevated Christian thought there remained a wide expansion which would cause this thought to penetrate the everyday life of the simple faithful. To this work, as difficult as the first, writers and preachers such as Richeome very soon dedicated themselves. But, in spite of these attempts, the Church, at the beginning of the seventeenth century, was still waiting for the genius who would perfectly realize this adaptation, this necessary vulgarization. Francis de Sales appeared, putting the whole Christian Renaissance within the grasp of the most humble in the form of little devotional books.

A doctoral dissertation has proved this work of Francis de Sales in minute detail: Francis de Sales, a serious student of the Jesuits, is a true humanist in the profane sense of the word, as were they who lived at the end of the Renaissance.[12] He did excellent studies in humanities; he had the classical authors, the Latin poets especially, at his fingertips. Francis himself wrote a beautiful Latin; stylized, effective and precious. This talent he put into his French style in the *Introduction to the Devout Life*, and subsequently into his more perfect *Treatise on the Love of God*. But that humanism, sometimes mistaken for a true humanism, will not be of any importance, at least for our purposes. The man, the director, the saint interests us more than the stylist, and this man is in effect one of the most striking in French history. To take this noble quality that the apostle is not afraid to apply to Christ, whatever we say of Francis de Sales, is summed up in his own statement, "I am too much a man to be more."[13] "And so — we only have a human heart and a natural sensitivity."[14] He adds elsewhere with greater precision: "I am not an extreme sort of man and I let myself willingly be carried away by change."[15] Give souls to lead to this type of man and he will write the *Introduction* for them. "Palmelius," as John P. Camus calls Francis de Sales in his novel *Parthenice*, "leads us to the kingdom of God with a beautifully flowering wreath full of sweet fruits of honor and gentleness."[16]

In spite of his strong attraction for Platonic speculation, he was professionally neither a philosopher nor a theologian. But he had read a great deal, reflected considerably on the dogmas which deal to a certain extent with the interior life and consequently direction; on the possibilities of fallen man; on nature and grace; on our relations with God. To convince oneself of this, one only has to read attentively the first books of the *Treatise on the Love of God*.

He expressly says in his preface:

The first four books and certain chapters in the others could
have been omitted for the sake of souls who seek only the
practice of holy charity...indeed, I have taken into account the
intellectual temper of our time, as was my duty. It is important
to keep in mind the age in which one writes.[17]

In this question of Christian humanism, it is enlightening to look
closely at the early Jesuit movement and indeed at Saint Ignatius. At the
beginning of his studies, in the city of Alcala, the future founder of the
Company of Jesus exposed himself to humanism only insofar as the latter was
necessary to understand the Fathers. In Paris, the teaching of Erasmus was
triumphing, trying to renew theology, penetrating it with the study of the
Bible.[18]

But how does one reconcile the Latin-Greek culture with the
exigencies of a good Christian formation? This difficulty and danger did not
escape the attention of the disciples of Saint Ignatius: "Several," writes
Father Richeome, in exposing these authors, either vocally, in the pulpit, or
with a pen, "are in their writings more profane than the profane people about
whom they comment, nastier than the authors of the knaveries that they are
exposing, more unfaithful than those whom they know have absolutely no
faith."[19]

In face of this danger, one tactic consisted of ignoring at least some of
the pagan authors:[20] "It is proper," said the partisans of this method, "to give
the place of honor to the doctors and the Fathers of the Church."[21] In favor
of their thesis, they invoked the famous dream of Saint Jerome, that Father
who best knew the pagan authors. The Jesuits replied in interpreting the
dream of Jerome: "The judge did not reproach Jerome for having
assiduously studied Cicero, but for having forgotten that he was Christian and
for having neglected the prophets."[22] The introduction of Christian classics
could not suffice; languages, like men, have their maturity: "The Fathers of
the Church, still more than Seneca, Tacitus or Statius were unfortunately
born too late."[23] Exception is made for the Greek fathers whom, in 1599,
were studied on a par "with Aesop, Plato and Thucydides." Furthermore, the
elevation of thoughts, expressed by the Fathers or the Christian poets,

rendered them nearly inaccessible to the child. "How, when an orator has so much trouble to make himself understood by mature men, when he speaks of things of God or when he explains the Fathers, could one pretend that, in class, children listen to the explanation of the same texts?"[24]

It was then necessary to find the middle way to incorprate both systems: first, to take from the pagan authors the truths they taught, and second, to refute the errors which were numerous. The pagans could be good moral professors. Saint Paul said that they understood the natural law by their conscience.[25] We can find examples of undeniable virtue among them: "Honor your father and your mother." Not only the law of grace, but the law of nature teaches us such a duty: Geneas, the Trojan captain, in saving Anchises his father, learns from this pagan, who calls himself Christian, how he ought to act toward his parents. We can then imitate the pagans "and take from them things which are good in themselves, such as several good natural acts, as honoring one's father and mother, to fast, to give alms or even some indifferent things, such as being dressed in such and such a way."[26]

However, there were dangers which had to be foreseen. No pagan philosopher taught the truth without mixing it with error. One would scarcely find in them any mention of humility; likewise poverty and virginity were objects of their scorn: thus one ought to teach the children only an antiquity well understood, or stripped of all that is libertinage or impiety.[27] "A well written work ordinarily allies the reader to the writer and this can produce in the author a certain authority due to the good that he has written. This in turn can serve to persuade his reader of something evil which he may write later."[28] Hence firmly, but without violence, Saint Ignatius discontinues in class the study of Vives and of Terence.[29] At Montaigu the reading of Terence, of Martial and of Juvenal was prohibited.[30] Pius IV and Gregory XIII highly approved this approach.[31] As a result, without going so far as to attribute to pagan fables a mystical sense, he had to fill in the gaps,[32] correct errors, study the passions according to Aristotle and construct a theodicy.[33]

Such was the method of Christian humanists. It could be very well applied to Stoicism.

Christian humanists considered Stoic truth as possessing a certain conformity with the Christian truths, since they have a common factor which is reason. By its high ideal of duty, by its domination of passions, by the invitation that it extends to accept a difficult life and to lead it without complaining about suffering, Stoicism lent itself admirably to the needs of souls. At this time men were absorbed with the pernicious evils provoked by the religious crises and the civil wars.

On the other hand, a reevaluation imposed itself. It was necessary first of all to show that this moral force in Stoicism was drawn not from itself, but from the strength of the Gospel. The highest moral theses of the Stoics were often only speculation for their pagan innovators, paradoxes in which they themselves sensed the emptiness. It is Christian wisdom which, in reconsidering them, has penetrated and embellished them. Still more, it is Ignatian spirituality which impregnated these doctrines. The Stoic believed only in human strength and let himself be misled by the devil of pride; he idealized the wise man who encloses himself in his ivory tower and who wills to depend on no one. Saint Ignatius and his followers attribute to human energy entirely different potentialities and quite a different orientation; they make humility the foundation and the pillar of all Christian virtues.[34] The Stoic strength is stripped of its arrogance and completely orientated toward God.

Hence two great principles dominate the work of Christian humanism: first, picking out the errors, secondly, utilizing the truths contained in Stoicism.

This method possesses a certain theological foundation, since original sin has not entirely corrupted human nature and pagans were capable of certain truths as of certain virtues. This spirit is found again in Marcus Antonius Muret, who, in publishing a critical edition of the complete works of Seneca,[35] shows that he considers it worthwhile for Christians to read and even study this Stoic philosopher. However, in his commentaries he often points out the errors and the dangers of Stoicism. Next a new spirit is born. Christian Stoicism takes its place along with humanism. This is an effort to bring about the canonization of Epictetus and Seneca. Some Christian writers hide the insufficiencies of these two philosophers. They interpret in a

Christian way their paradoxes and little by little they slip toward a secularization of Christianity or even toward a pure and simple naturalism. Such is the position of both professor Justus Lipsus and of the politician Guillaume du Vair. During this time, Michel de Montaigne begins by writing according to the taste of the period and becomes stoically obdurate in the course of a crisis and under the influence of Plutarch and of Sextus Empiricus. He burns what he adored and criticizes pitilessly the stoic moral. Finally, establishing his personal morality, he continues his criticism of Stoicism at the same time that he exploits the psychological riches of Seneca; hence he uses once more the method of Christian humanism, but in a new way. During all this evolution, Christian humanism was not silent. The Jesuit Delrio comments on the tragedies of Seneca without losing sight of the fact that at certain times they can be very useful and at other times very dangerous. The Jacobin John of St. Francis, in translating Epictetus, vaunts him a little more than he should. But in his praise of Nicolas Lefevre, he recalls the beautiful virtue of humility which was undoubtedly not practiced by the author of the *Manual*. St. Francis de Sales came into direct contact with Epictetus through the translation of John of St. Francis and he shows a marked affection for this wise man of antiquity. Seneca and the other Stoics, however, he could have known only through Saint Augustine. Continuing the method advocated by Saint Ignatius and his disciples, he shows the insufficiency and the dangers of Stoicism and teaches how to enhance the virtues that this philosophical sect has been able to practice naturally; he also gives in his method a theological foundation – nature not being completely corrupted but rather presenting some possibilities, that we shall call passive, of supernatural elevation.

Hence we shall see that Saint Francis de Sales will be a "spirit of his century." Sometimes in his works we shall find some Christian Stoicism as it is practiced by a number of very fervent Christians. But his works will be of a Christian humanist style which occupies a middle position, distinguishing in Stoicism the good and the bad, utilizing one and deleting the other.

An exhaustive study of the scholarly sources of Francis de Sales is probably impossible He read very much, and of all his correspondence, which could give us precious clues to the extent of his learning, only an infinitesimally small part has come down to us today. It would be necessary, in order to render less aleatory this overall view, that one have studied the influence of Saint Augustine, Saint Bernard, Pseudo-Dionysius, and many others. It would be negligent not to mention the monumental study done by A. Liuima on the sources of *The Treatise on Divine Love*. We shall refer to it since it is the only general study which has been written on this subject.

Here we are especially interested in the sources of Francis' Stoicism. Doubtless, Francis de Sales' knowledge of the great Latin and Greek doctors was drawn from the best accessible sources of his day. Historians tell us that he was attached essentially to the Jesuits of Clermont College, who had formed and enriched him with ancient culture and gave him a taste for things of the mind. From the humanists of the Renaissance, he had learned his beautiful style, and a delight for letters and arts; but his ideas derive from the Christian Middle Ages; that is, writings profoundly penetrated with the Gospel. Paganism does not effect him, unlike so many of his precursors who only write of muses, fairies, nymphs, Venus or Cypris. For example, Pierre de Ronsard and Pierre Charron prefer pagan writings over the evangelical truths. These men have nearly lost faith, hope and the Christian sense of life while in contact with pagan ideas of sensuality, Epicureanism and certainly Stoicism. As a consequence, Pierre Charron and Guillaume du Vair secularize the moral that they found on reason. Pierre Charron's wisdom is a somber fatalism when confronting fundamental questions. His humanism degrades man.

On the contrary, beginning with the ancients, Francis is enriched, broadened and rises toward his ideal. "No more, no less" is stated on the coat of arms of his ancestors. While he assimilates the true values of the ancients, he foregoes their vanities.

Undoubtedly, he owes his knowledge of Stoicism in large part to Saint Augustine (*The City of God*), but he read Seneca and Epictetus, especially the latter "whose words and opinions are so pleasing to read in our language in the translation that the learned and graceful pen of the Reverend Father Dom John of Saint Francis, Provincial of the Congregation of Feuillants among the Gauls, has recently made available for our reading."[36] In these lines is not simply the accidental compliment to the able translator who renders "pleasing" the harsh sentences of the original. The Bishop honors Epictetus as "that good man" of all paganism who won his heart. Struck by the nobility of the maxims, St. Francis goes so far as to conjecture: "He expressed the wish to die as a true Christian, as he very probably did."[37] This is a particular evidence of the attraction exercised on the first Christian generations and which would suggest to them a manner of generous annexation. As Tertullian said, *Seneca saepe noster.* Conjecture aside, one could not overlook the praise intended for the pagan philosopher, an expression of respect and admiration, which, in various degrees, reflects again the Stoic and philosophical tradition of antiquity. Better than all others, in the eyes of Francis de Sales, Epictetus expresses the will to liberate the soul, to free it from all enslaving subjection. This exalted and exalting will could not, first of all, contradict any moralist who, on a different level, stressed the major importance of the will. The disdain of material goods, the exclusive search for interior liberty and moral perfection, appeared praiseworthy "in Epictetus more than in any other philosopher" since in his writing a religious sentiment of submission to God (or gods) accompanied a happy and unreserved acceptance of the law of providence (or destiny). The principal theses or the principal Stoic themes caught the attention and the consideration of a bishop concerned with guaranteeing the purity of ecclesiastical doctrine but who was not against new ideas. Does the source of the ideas or the resemblance of attitudes permit us to suppose a penetration of Stoicism in Salesian thought? Is this conclusion not confirmed by the use of idioms or expressions that one might normally come upon in the *Manual, The Letters to Lucilius* and the *Introduction to the Devout Life*? "The great happiness of man is to possess his soul"?[38] In Chapter Seven of the third part we find: "We must prefer the fruit before the leaves, namely, interior and spiritual graces before all external goods." Further, the *Introduction* states: "Resolve to surrender to Him whatever is most dear to you whenever it shall please Him to take it: father, mother, brother, husband, wife, child, even your eyes and your life. For all these sacrifices ought you to prepare your heart."[39]

Does the *Introduction* not repeat a Stoic notion (inherited from Socrates)[40] when it sees the cause of sin in ignorance? Does it not reiterate the cry already made by ancient wisdom when it proclaims that the whole world is not worth a resolute soul?[41]

One wonders if such analogies suggested to Brunetière the simultaneously categoric and vague statement of the *Manual* presenting the *Introduction* as a Stoic book – or almost.[42] References to truncated citations and ideas detached from an integral whole may greatly mislead others. Recourse to texts and to contexts prevents error due to the arbitrary splitting up of sentences, and overdue attention paid to words rather than intelligent interpretation.[43]

The "possession of his soul" is an expression from the psalmist without profane reference in Francis de Sales; it is only the first stage of obedience to revealed law which is necessarily balanced by another: "Alas, what am I when I am my own?"[44] The first notion, which seems to satisfy the proprietary instinct of the individual, mentally provokes the second which recognizes the need of being expropriated. One must belong to oneself in order to give oneself.[45]

The manner in which one accepts suffering and death is understood only in the light of fundamental beliefs, of a whole gamut of ideas and sentiments whose unity cannot be disturbed and which determines its true nature. These ideas and sentiments, in the course of a sacerdotal life rich in observations, experiences and reflections, grow more precise and take on various nuances in order that they be communicated. But the essentials do not change. They characterize in a continuous way the Salesian spirituality. The *Introduction to the Devout Life* is not more Stoic than the *Treatise on the Love of God*. The criticisms formulated in the former concerning Stoicism could be inserted equally well in the latter.

Thus the bishop and prince of Geneva is in the tradition of great Christian humanists. But there is more than continuity and good neighborliness in the saint of devout and mystical humanism. In him humanism is a way of being in the world, with people like him and with God, a way of being which colors everything he is and everything he writes. In him, the sentiment of nature, philosophy and culture, moral and religious life, public good works as well as his intimate letters, are marked constantly by this humanism which completely impregnates the man.

On the occasion of the death of a niece, Francis says of himself: "I am too much a man to be more."[46] Special significance can be accorded to such an expression pronounced in a moment of great sorrow. It is certain that he never denied his humanity.

The humanism of Francis de Sales is perhaps nowhere better expressed than in this page written to the glory of the body.

> Charity places an obligation upon us to love our bodies properly, since they are necessary for good works, constitute part of our person, and will share in eternal happiness. Indeed, a Christian must love his body as a living image of his incarnate Savior, as having issued with him from the same stock, and consequently belonging to him in parentage and blood. Above all, this holds after we have renewed the alliance by the real reception of the divine body of our Redeemer in the most adorable sacrament of the Eucharist, and after we have dedicated and consecrated ourselves to supreme goodness by baptism, confirmation, and other sacraments.[47]

While unreserved in his approval of the body, this bishop, in the tradition of Christian humanists, finds in pagan antiquity both good and bad: we can take some and we can leave some.

There is some bad, and the author of the *Treatise on Divine Love* does not hesitate to point it out. What he reproaches in Stoicism, from the dogmatic point of view, is not its having admitted but its having preached the plurality of the gods. "See what a pity it is," says he in regard to Epictetus, "to watch this excellent philosopher at times speak of God in the pagan way." What Epictetus lacked was "a holy jealousy of God's honor so as not to err or dissemble in a matter of such great importance."[48] He makes the same reproach of Seneca and even more virulently: he wrote a book entitled *Against Superstitions*, in which he criticized pagan impiety with great freedom. "This freedom," says the great Saint Augustine, "is found in his writings but not in his life," since he even advised "that men should put superstition out of their hearts but not give up its natural practice." These are his words: "The sage should observe such superstitions because they are commanded by law not because they are pleasing to the gods."[49]

From the moral point of view, Saint Francis de Sales reproaches the Stoics primarily because of their in sensitivity. In a letter to Saint Jeanne de Chantal, he declares that "this imaginary insensitiveness of those who do not wish to suffer as man, has always seemed a true chimera."[50] Elsewhere Saint Francis makes a judgment which has much more nuance; he recognizes the Stoic doctrine that the wise man who must not have passions, can still have affections. "They were not wrong," said he, "in holding that there are eupathies or good affections"; he reproaches them however for denying "that the wise man, could ever feel sadness, whereas no evil can befall the wise man, for according to their principles no one is ever injured except by himself...." "They were wrong," he wrote, "in the sensual part, and that sadness cannot affect the heart of the wise man; because, leaving aside the fact that they themselves were troubled by them, how could wisdom deprive us of pity? Pity is virtuous sorrow...Epictetus always escapes this reproach, because," according to Saint Augustine, "he did not fall into this error that passions do not rise up in the wise man."[51] In the *Treatise on the Love of God*, he says that "as for the virtues that our neighbor, the pagans trod them under foot and by their very laws trampled most shamefully on the chief of them, which is piety;" among other examples of the severity, he cites that of Seneca, "that sage so highly praised," who insisted that one kill monsters and who admitted without reserve the abandon of defective, feeble, imperfect or monstrous children.[52]

Another reproach from the moral point of view is that of vanity or rather pride. Simplicity is specifically a Christian virtue:[53] "Pagans, even the most eloquent on the subject of the other virtues, knew nothing whatever of this, any more than of humility. They wrote exceedingly well on liberality and constancy, but of simplicity and humility they have written nothing at all."[54] In a letter to Celse Bènigne de Chantal, Saint Francis advised this young man not to "desire virtue attained by means of philosophy," because these are only "shadow-figures of virtue."[55]

But, inasmuch as they are shadow-figures, these acts of virtue are not less imitable, certainly not in the intention which commands them, but in what they are in themselves. In fact, Saint Francis de Sales mentions occasionally to his Christian readers the example of virtues exercised by some Stoics. Seneca and Plutarch recommend the examination of conscience. The former in particular speaks convincingly of interior trouble that remorse excites in the soul. Epictetus describes the self-reprehension that we must practice and he expresses the hope of dying a true Christian, and it is probable that he finally did.[56] Furthermore, this same sage, by a very extreme renunciation, did not wish his liberty, but remained voluntarily in such abject slavery that after his death they found nothing belonging to him but a lamp.[57] Saint Francis de Sales goes so far as to say: "If you want to sanctify the human and moral virtues of Epictetus, Socrates, or Demades, simply have them practiced by some truly Christian soul, that is by one who possesses love of God."[58] Here is a more detailed analysis of this transposition: "The Stoics, particularly good Epictetus, placed all their philosophy in this: to abstain and to sustain; to forbear and to bear up under; to abstain from and to forbear earthly pleasures, delights, and honors; and to sustain and bear up under injuries, labors, and troubles. Christian doctrine, the sole true philosophy, has three principles on which it bases all its practices – self-denial, which is far more than to abstain from pleasures; to carry Christ's cross, which is far more than to lift it up; to follow our Lord, not only in renouncing self and in carrying his cross, but also in whatever belongs to the practice of every kind of good work."[59]

This transposition, or rather this elevation from Stoicism to Christianity, possible with the aid of grace, is founded in the humanism of Saint Francis de Sales. Man is not entirely perverted by original sin; next to misery, there is a place in him for a certain grandeur which will be able to serve as a point of departure for an ascension toward the supernatural world. The will possesses an inclination to love God above all things,[60] a natural inclination which of itself does not permit us to love God as we ought,[61] but which is nonetheless very useful because God uses it as a handle, in order more easily to take us and draw us to himself.[62]

Reason is a good tree that God has planted in us; whose fruits can only be good.[63] Undoubtedly the spirit is sick; it is seriously wounded and as if half dead; it perceives the commandments and cannot obey them. But God esteems virtues, even though they are practiced by some persons who are also bad; the apostle assures us that pagans who lack faith, do by nature what the law prescribes. When they do so, who can doubt that they act well and that God takes it into account?[64] Hence, in a very ineffective way, distant but very real, Stoicism, or rather the Stoics, will be able, to a certain degree, to be utilized by Christians; it will be necessary to empty them of their pride and to vivify them by love.

We shall see in the following chapters some virtues as they are presented in the works of Saint Francis de Sales. We shall notice, first of all, how indifference exists in a completely different form in Saint Francis from that in the Stoics. Next we shall briefly consider a synthesis of Salesian spirituality and virtues which will give us a clear idea of the spirit which is entirely Christian and was that of Saint Francis de Sales.

Chapter I Endnotes

1 Zanta, L., *La renaissance du stoicisme au XVIIe siècle*, Paris, Champion, 1914.

2 *Preparation evangelique*, XIV, 5, 4.

3 *Discourses*, I, 16.

4 *La Volante de Puissance*, p. 357.

5 *Entretien avec M. de Saci sur Epictete et Montaigne*, Brunschvicg, p. 150.

6 *Discourses*, II, 16, 28; III, 7.

7 *Ibid.*, II, 16.

8 Horace, *Odes*, III, 3, 7-8.

9 *Ibid.*

10 Saint Gregory the Great, *Expositiones in Librum Primum Regum*, V, 3.

11 Bremond, H., *A Literary History of Religious Thought in France*, trans. K. L. Montgomery, New York, Macmillan, 1936, II, p. 13.

12 Delplanque, A., *Saint François de Sales, humaniste et ecrivain latin*, Lille, 1907.

13 *Oeuvres*, XIII, p. 330 [Stopp, p. 141].

14 *Ibid.*, XIV, p. 264.

15 *Ibid.*, p. 39.

16 *Parthenice*, p. 333.

17 *Oeuvres*, IV, p. 9 [Ryan, I, p. 41].

18 DeDainville, F., s.j., *La naissance de l'humanisme moderne*, Paris, Beauchesne, 1940.

19 *Ibid.*, p. 210

20 *Ibid.*, p. 211 ff.

21 *Ibid.*, p. 214.

22 *Ibid.*, p. 215.

23 *Ibid.*, p. 216.

24 *Ibid.*, p. 217.

25 *Ibid.*, p. 223 ff.

26 *Ibid.*, p. 226.

27 *Ibid.*, p. 229.

28 St. Ignatius, *Epistle IX*, 1555, cited in F. DeDainville, *op. cit.*, p. 229.

29 *Ibid.*, p. 230.

30 *Loc. cit.*

31 *Loc. cit.*

32 *Ibid.*, p. 233.

33 *Ibid.*, p. 237.

34 *Vide infra*, II, p. 50 ff.

35 Muret, M. A., *Opera*, Ruhnken, 1789.

36 *Ibid.*, IV, p. 81 ff. [Ryan, I, p. 96].

37 *Ibid.*, p. 148 [Ryan, I, p. 149].

38 *Ibid.*, III, p. 133 [Ryan, p. 124].

39 *Ibid.*, III, p. 254 [Ryan, p. 207].

40 *Ibid.*, p. 235 ff. [Ryan, p. 193 ff.].

41 *Ibid.*, p. 359 [Ryan, p. 282].

42 *Manuel de L'Histoire de la Litterature française*, p. 99.

43 Spannuel, M., *Le Stoicisme des Pères de l'Eglise*, pp. 250, 257.

44 *Ibid.*, III, p. 325 ff.

45 We readily admit, though reserving an intrepretation to which we shall refer below, that the Stoic submits himself, but does not give himself nor sacrifice himself out of love.

46 *Oeuvres*, XIII, p. 30.

22

47   *Ibid.*, IV, p. 192 ff. [Ryan, p. 183 ff.].

48   *Ibid.*, p. 82 [Ryan, I, p. 96 ff.].

49   *Ibid.*, V, p. 270 [Ryan, II, p. 223].

50   *Ibid.*, XIV, p. 163.

51   *Ibid.*, IV, p. 36 ff. [Ryan, I, p. 63 ff.].

52   *Ibid.*, V, p. 271 ff. [Ryan, II, p. 224].

53   *Vide infra*, III, p. 85 ff.

54   *Ibid.*, VI, p. 203 [Gasquet, p. 215 ff.].

55   *Ibid*, XIV, p. 378 [Stopp, p. 188].

56   *Ibid.*, p. 148 [Ryan, I, p. 149].

57   *Ibid.*, VI, p. 23 [Gasquet, p. 20].

58   *Ibid.*, V, p. 241 [Ryan, II, p. 200].

59   *Ibid.*, p. 113 [Ryan, II, p. 100 ff.].

60   *Ibid.*, IV, p. 74 [Ryan, I, p. 141].

61   *Ibid.*, p. 80 [*Ibid.*, p. 145 ff.].

62   *Ibid.*, p. 83 [*Ibid.*, p. 148 ff.].

63   *Ibid.*, I, pp. 330-32.

64   *Ibid.*, V, p. 237 [Ryan, II, p. 197].

CHAPTER II

True Abandon according to Saint Francis de Sales

In the works of Saint Francis de Sales, doctor of indifference, the Christian can become very well informed on the subject of coping with suffering. This great humanist and doctor of the Church shows remarkably well how the Christian can be sanctified through a certain kind of spiritual indifference. Saint Francis teaches us that we must unite our will with that of God in such a way that his and ours are one.

> There is absolutely no doubt that the suffering which can sometimes be a stimulant for the spiritual life is very often an obstacle. Suffering is profitable only when it is overcome, when it is accepted by a will which has perfect control of itself. Oriental spiritual authors have spoken at considerable length of *apatheia*, that disposition of the soul victorious over suffering and passions, which bathes the soul in tranquility even during its moments of greatest sorrow. But if the word is of Stoic origin – it points out in the Stoic the suppression of every violent sentiment, pleasure and desire – the Christian sense has taken on a more human and more divine meaning.[1]

St. Francis views the will of God as being manifested in two general ways: "The will of God is either the declared will, that which is known in advance, manifested clearly and explicitly by the commandments of God and of the Church, the Evangelical Counsels, inspirations, and the Rules and Constitutions,"[2] vows and orders of superiors; or the will of God's good pleasure "which we must regard in all events and circumstances that may befall us. In sickness and death, in affliction, and consolation, in things adverse and in things prosperous; in short, in all the unforeseen occurrences of life."[3]

To submit to the declared will of God is not abandon or passivity but rather obedience. However, there are events that depend upon God's good pleasure and these are the proper subjects of abandon. Indeed, this latter area is an immense one. Because even where the declared will of God comes about, there still remains this possibility of abandon. "One must work with zeal for the success of an enterprise that one prudently considers inspired by God and then peacefully accept the defeat, if God wills that it be thus."[4] But there cannot be opposition between the declared will of God and his will of good pleasure. They necessarily are in accord.

If there is an apparent conflict, it is the declared will of God which gives sense to the second: "for of course to it obedience must take precedence,"[5] according to the Bishop of Geneva. To resign oneself, in the actual sense of the word, is not yet to abandon oneself. Abandon requires a more generous gift of self than a kind of forced acceptance or almost constrained acquiescence which is accompanied by deliberation and hesitation.

Certain people consider indifference a negative virtue and a step along the way to abandon. Hence the indifference described in the early meditation of the *Exercises* of Saint Ignatius is certainly a preliminary disposition to abandon: it supposes the human will in a state of awaiting the divine will, the soul prepared to act at that moment when it perceives the good pleasure of God; but indifference no longer has any reason for its being, once the will of the good pleasure of God is manifested. Hence, according to Saint Francis, it is so intimately united to abandon that he normally calls it "holy indifference." In the second *Conference*, he defines it as "the acceptance with perfect indifference of all the events which may befall us, just as they arrive by the order of God's providence: affliction equally with consolation, sickness as health, poverty as riches, contempt as honor, shame as glory."[6] In Book Nine of the *Love of God* which treats of "The love of submission, by which our will is united to God's good pleasure," he distinguishes only between resignation and indifference: "Resignation prefers God's will above all things, yet it does not cease to love many other things in addtion to God's will. Indifference goes beyond resignation, for it loves nothing except for love of God's will so that nothing touches the indifferent heart in the presence of God's will."[7] Saint Francis de Sales does not oppose holy indifference to abandon. He simply identifies abandon with perfect indifference.

Indifference or abandon, as he understands it, is the perfect equilibrium of the soul in awaiting the manifestation of divine orders; it can therefore only be exercised in cases where the will of God has not taken on some definite form: At that moment, indifference becomes a joyful acceptance, a loving and eager obedience.

What has been said thus far in no way conflicts with chapter fifteen of the Ninth Book of the *Treatise*. By this comparison the author presents us a human will in a first attitude of abandon and absolute confidence. But once the more explicit expression of the divine will takes place, immediately the waiting will succeeds the personal movement of the soul. In just this way the sick little girl, certain of her father's desire, not only accepted his care, but took every means required in order to hasten her acquiring good health. As the saint has said elsewhere: "You must always then submit to what is asked of you in order to do the will of God, provided it be not contrary to that will, as signified to you."[8] Now, "to will as God" is generally to will two times, since this is to will against our instinct, although for St. Francis this instinct can coincide with the divine will. To renounce oneself is to be oneself. It is to strip oneself of interior and instinctive movements which tyrannize us. It is to be liberated from capricious actions. To strangle one's blind fantasies is to strengthen one's personality, to establish in oneself the control of the will, of a will adopted to God's. The Bishop of Geneva very clearly saw this identity of holy indifference and liberty: "That is why," he wrote to Madame de Chantal, "it is necessary to acquire the spirit of holy liberty and indifference as much as possible."[9] In the state of indifference, in effect, one is no longer dominated by life; one dominates it. And the Salesian acceptation, far from leading to the Buddhist ataraxia or a Wertherian fatalism, develops, on the contrary, one's initiative by making a constant appeal to a voluntary effort. "If you will examine this matter," says Saint Francis de Sales, "this waiting on the part of the soul is truly voluntary...and as soon as the events take place and are received, the waiting changes into consent or acquiescence."[10] This consent seems to him so penetrated with the "voluntary" that he hesitates to name it "acceptation," a word which seems ambiguous to him, "because to accept and receive are actions that to a certain extent might be called 'passive actions.'"[11] It is a simple question of a word. Besides, whatever the name might be that we give to the mental attitude advocated by the Bishop of Geneva, whether we call it acceptation, indifference or abandon, it always implies for him an effort on our part, an act of cooperation, an endeavor toward adhesion. It is a voluntary acceptance, indifference or abandon. It has nothing in common with the chimeric "apathy" dreamed of by the Stoic. The Salesian does not say: "I abandon myself as prey to the laws of the universe." To the ancient formula *sustine* he adds a positive element of love which transforms it. He says: "To carry Christ's cross is far more than to lift it up."[12] He says further: "Resignation is practiced by way of effort and submission."[13] To accept then is not to be abandoned, it is to take oneself in hand, if we can express it this way, and, by a virile and loyal effort, to adapt ourselves to the order fixed by God. It is by constant appeal to the will that Saint Francis de Sales leads us to holy indifference.

Abandon, like all Christian virtues, has its source in the Gospel, in the teachings and examples of our Lord Jesus Christ. Saint Francis de Sales several times has represented to us Christ as a model of abandon at various points in his mortal life,[14] during his early childhood,[15] during the flight into Egypt,[16] but especially during the sorrows throughout his life and his passion by these incomparable words: "Father, I abandon my spirit into your hands."[17] The imitation of our Lord here again is the great moving force of souls: how many have abandoned themselves to the will of God in their suffering while repeating the words that their Saviour pronounced in the garden of Olives: "Not my will, but thine be done."[18] "Nevertheless not as I will, but as thou wilt."[19] There is nothing more reasonable than abandon to the good pleasure of God. We see in it the natural agreement of reason with its principle. God, being sovereign master, will always accomplish His will in spite of ours.

The resignation of the Stoics approached very close to a veritable abandon to providence. Epictetus was almost practicing it when Arrian made him say: "We must make the best use that we can of the things that are in our power, and use the rest according to their nature. What is their nature then? As God may please."[20] It seems that the Stoics tried to balance perfectly the action of man and the action of the divinity in their life by a well-known distinction. That is, there are those things which depend on us and those which do not depend on us. By the resolution of these, one was to submit perfectly to that which God willed: "Wherefore the wise and good man, remembering who he is and whence he came, and by whom he was produced, is attentive only to this, how he may fill his place with due regularity, and obediently to God."[21] Everything for Epictetus was an occasion, as he said, "to be in conformity with the will of nature." For him this conformity was Mercury's wand which changed into gold everything that it touched. Saint Francis de Sales speaks of those "ancient philosophers who have performed admirable abandonment of everything and of themselves for a vain pretension and in order to give themselves to philosophy."[22] Would that they had added a more coherent doctrine on God and his love so that one could speak of their abandon. Saint Francis himself warns us that it is the author of the *Exercises* who is his master regarding this point: "Father Ignatius Loyola, whom they are going to canonize on Ash Wednesday, ate meat on doctor's orders. The latter judged this expedient for a little sickness with which Ignatius was taken. A spirit of constraint caused him to pray over this for three days."[23] The Bishop of Geneva had understood St. Ignatius.

It is also certain that Francis was inspired by St. Theresa of Avila. It is possible that, in order to make his teaching very clear, Francis searched for some examples and comparisons in the writings of the holy reformer. On the other hand, this may have been an unconscious imitation which would explain why Theresa was not cited. Then we could derive this from Francis himself, and use it to characterize his literary debt to St. Theresa in the beautiful comparison that he uses in order to describe he love of conformity. "It is strange but true that when two lutes in unison, that is, with the same sound and pitch, are placed close together and someone plays one of them, then although the other is untouched it will not keep from sounding just like the one played on. The adaptation of one to the other is like natural love and produces this correspondence."[24]

Studying the historical development of the Salesian doctrine of holy indifference, Pierre Veuillot points out that this doctrine appears in Saint Francis de Sales as early as 1602, but that it is enriched continually right up to the *Treatise on the Love of God.* Thus Veuillot notes in the first letters of direction:

> The perspectives are more restrained than they will be in the *Treatise*; the virtue of indifference is still conceived by him in direct reference with the acceptance of sufferings, while later he will present it to us as a more general and more positive attitude of soul, an attitude of exclusive love of God penetrating every pain and every joy.[25]

Was this enlargement of the concept of indifference, between 1606 and 1616 when Saint Francis de Sales advanced in his knowledge of St. Theresa, not a result of his own spiritual progress? In his own development, he gradually perceived that indifference is not a state which must endure, but rather is the "balance that holds the scales at rest": a balance which necessarily must be upset if the scale is to serve a purpose. It is simply a given condition, a transitory state in which the will is in temporary equilibrium it must abstain from taking sides, as long as it does not know God's preference. But Veuillot justly emphasizes that Salesian indifference is something more: "The treatises on spirituality willingly consider indifference as a negative virtue, a simple step of the soul toward an attitude of filial and abandoned love."[26]

Such is the teaching of Saint Ignatius and sometimes also that of Saint Francis de Sales. However it is much more than a preliminary and negative disposition that is taught in Book Nine of the *Treatise.* In reality, Saint Francis de Sales identifies abandon and pure love with perfect indifference and this is what gives value to this important virtue in his spirituality. The virtue of indifference resumes, in the eyes of Saint Francis de Sales, all of Christian perfection. The resignation of the *Imitation* of Jesus Christ is half-way between abnegation and the gift of self, or rather it is an amalgamation of the two: *De pura et integra resignatione sui ad obtiniendam cordis libertatem.*[27] Abandon, as described by Saint Francis de Sales, coincides as well with abnegation and giving oneself to God: "You must know that to practice self-abandonment and to forsake ourselves, is nothing else but to yield up and get rid of our own will that we may give it to God."[28] This detachment extends even to desires: "We must neither ask anything nor refuse anything, but leave ourselves in the arms of divine Providence, without busying ourselves with any desires, except to will what God wills of us."[29] In order to attach oneself to God, one must be completely unattached. The divine good pleasure sometimes appears absolute and irrevocable: we retain the right to form desires and prayers. But detachment, faith in providence and confidence in God are only the beginning of abandon. In order that it be complete, in order to give oneself unreservedly to God, love is requisite. Saint Francis de Sales writes concerning this point: "Almost everyone can manage to trust God in the sweetness of peace and prosperity; but only his children can put their trust in him when storms and tempests rage, I mean put their trust in him with complete self-abandonment."[30] Love is indispensable by its very end – which is to unite us to God, and it is hence useless and vain for the ancient philosophers.[31] Abandon leads to the perfection of holy love, at the same time that it permits the soul to express its love. We can say with equal exactitude that man must love in order to abandon himself and abandon himself in order to love. Abandon is the most complete expression of perfect love.

In chapter five of Book Nine, Francis de Sales shows "that holy indifference extends to all things."[32] The examples given show very clearly that he does not limit the concept of indifference as does St Ignatius in the *Exercises*. It is no longer a question of "keeping the scale balanced" in order to know God's will without any risk of error. But God's will once being known, as with Job on the dung pile or Christ on the cross, the loving soul remains absolutely of one mind with Him. The following chapter treats "of the practice of loving indifference as to things belonging to God's service."[33] Francis borrows from the lives of the saints several traits destined to bring out the fact that "to train us in such holy indifference God very often inspires us with lofty plans but does not will that they succeed."[34] Again, in chapter nine, Francis develops the famous apology of the deaf musician who continues to sing in spite of his infirmity. Without the pleasure of hearing his own melody nor even the pleasure of pleasing his absent prince, he continues singing merely from the pure desire of obeying the will of his master.[35] Francis uses this example to teach pure love or, as he calls it here, "the purity of indifference." The deafness, which still permits the singer to please his prince, is the symbol of spiritual dryness. And the absence of the prince, who "having ordered him to sing, would retire or go out hunting, taking neither the leisure to hear him nor the pleasure of hearing him,"[36] signifies in figurative language that "great suffering" which the soul experiences when, during the mystical night, it undergoes the cruel experience of the absence of God.

Francis de Sales consecrates the last chapters of the Ninth Book to the "Most lovable death of the will."[37] He likewise establishes a perfect parallelism between Books Six and Seven (on the love of indifference) which conclude with the "death of love"; and Books Eight and Nine, which, dealing with the love of pleasure, terminate with that penetrating study of the supreme degree of conformity and of indifference, which is the death of the will. The spiritual trials can attain to such a degree of acuity that the soul no longer feels the virtues that are in it: "Hence it thinks that it has no faith, no hope, no love."[38] Love takes refuge "in the very summit and supreme region of the spirit." The soul "has no further power except to let its will die in the hands of God's will," and to say with Christ on the cross: "Alas, O my Father, into your hands I commend my spirit."[39]

He explains this mystical death of the will in the following manner: "Our will in fact can never die, no more than our soul can, yet sometimes it passes over the boundaries of its accustomed life so as to live wholly in the divine will.... What becomes of the light of the stars when the sun appears on the horizon? Such light does not actually perish, but it is ravished and absorbed into the sun's supreme light with which it is happily intermingled and joined."[40] Saint Francis had employed an analagous image in order to describe the union, not the prayer of union of which he so often speaks, but the infinitely more intimate and permanent union: "...the will that is dead to itself so as to live in God's will is without any particular desire, and remains not only in conformity and subjection but it's totally annihilated in itself and is converted into God's will."[41] And as his imagination is incontestably rich, he makes use of it in order to make his thought understood with very beautiful images, such as "the heart that is embarked in the divine good pleasure" and should let itself "be moved solely by the motion of the vessel."[42] But the most beautiful and the most exact is still an ultimate development of the image of the child at his mother's breast: "It is like what might be said of a little child who does not yet have use of its will so as to desire or love anything except its dear mother's breast and face. It does not think of wanting to be on one side or the other, or of desiring anything else whatever save only to be in the arms of its mother, with whom it thinks it to be one being. It is never at pains to adapt its will to its mother's, for it does not know its own will and does not think it has one. To its mother it leaves complete care to go, to do, and to will what she finds good for it."[43]

It is well to will what God wills. It is better to leave the willing to God, contenting oneself to thank him for what he wills.[44] But it is still better to "divert our heart and fix our attention on God's goodness and sweetness, blessing it not in its effects and in the events it ordains but in itself and in its own perfection,"[45] which Francis illustrates in another equally famous narration: the daughter of the surgeon who, sick, confides herself totally to her father.[46] Surrender to God's will is the attitude recommended by him whom many have wished to consider as the precursor of the modern will theorists. "It is very difficult to put into exact words this highest indifference of the human will, which is thus reduced to God's will and has perished in it."[47] To acquiesce, accept, receive, permit; Saint Francis de Sales rejects each of these terms which still imply a certain activity of the will. "It seems to me that the soul that is in this state of indifference and wills nothing but leaves it to God to will what is pleasing to him must be said to have its will in a simple and general state of waiting. To wait is neither to do nor to act, but only to remain subject to some event. If you will examine the matter, this waiting on the part of the soul is truly voluntary. Nevertheless it is not an action but rather a simple disposition to receive whatever shall happen. As soon as the events take place and are received, the waiting changes into consent or acquiescence. But before they occur, the soul is truly in a state of simple waiting, indifferent to all the divine will is pleased to ordain."[48] Here we are at the summit of the Salesian doctrine of pure love; it is here especially that is shown the profound originality in his doctrine of total indifference. In truth, St. Francis has advanced and considerably developed this traditional tenet of spiritual life. He has expressed it in a systematic way. He has intimately lived it himself. Hence it is very much his own.

In a final chapter, Saint Francis de Sales presents the same doctrine of pure love, or of total indifference, or of perfect abandon – expressions practically synonomous – with the aid of a new image, "despoliation."[49] The image and action found in this word are ones familiar to him: in the Year 1616, when he was putting the finishing touches on the *Treatise*, he liked to present to Saint Chantal the immense sacrifice that he asked of her in their holy friendship under the figure of despoliation.[50] The origin of this metaphor is clearly scriptural and indeed the chapter opens with the representation of the naked Christ on the cross. Furthermore it has some roots in the Old Testament. Francis also evokes the spouse of the Canticles, Job and Judith.

But spiritual bareness is not an end in itself, as the quietists thought in recommending total passivity. Francis, on the contrary, had already expressed his famous and significant beatitude: "Blessed are they who have stripped their own heart, for Our Lord will clothe them."[51] He develops this idea in this chapter of the Treatise:

> We cannot long remain in such nakedness, stripped of every kind of affection. Hence, according to the advice of the holy Apostle, after we have put off the garments of the old Adam, we must put on the clothing of the new man, that is of Jesus Christ. Having renounced all things, yes, even affection for virtue we must clothe ourselves anew with various affections ...but...because they are agreeable to God...that is to say that they will not be used for themselves, but will bring all things back to the unique end of man: the service of God by the complete accomplishment of his will.

> The creature's want of application, that is ataraxy, is truly that 'total nudity' which renders the soul capable of an 'immediate union'; this is 'a spirit of death in which God places us' and 'does not permit that we desire anything except with indifference.'[52]

Indifference is purification and simplification of the state of anticipation. This virtue tends toward the dismissal of all human affection.

toward the absence of every concept or simply being conscious of its proper limits and accepting them, happy only to know that God exists: "...in a word, I live without life, I exist without being, God is and lives and that suffices for me...." as writes Bernières.[53]

However at this moment the danger is great. One may never insist enough on the part of Saint Francis in the genesis of that animosity which animates the French spiritual writers of the seventeenth century against the "sensitive." It is commonplace to insist on the mildness of the Bishop of Geneva. Louis Lavelle[54] recalls his virile conscience and his exaltation of will. However, it would seem, at least at the initial encounter, that there was opposition between will and love, since love is basically submission to the divine attraction and the will is generally conceived of as the affirmation of self; Saint Francis de Sales will unite these two aspirations in the one and same act, hence including himself in the Augustinian perspective according to which the will is in fact the desire for the Good, that is, the love of God.

Does not that which is proper to the will also oblige us to go out of ourselves, as if we found nothing in ourselves which was capable of satisfying us? And inversely, is it not we who love, and must we not say of love that it is what expresses the most hidden and the most intimate of our essence? Is it possible to will anything that one does not love? And there where love is present, am I not in the very act of willing, beyond that of willing, as if the will was surpassed and rendered useless? On this point Louis Lavelle concludes: but then there must be a point in ourselves the most profound will is confounded with the most hidden love.

This is precisely what we call the sentiment of indifference. If the will permits us to make it our own, this obscure power of love which infinitely surpasses our limits, of what importance is it, properly spoken, to "feel" it? Hence the saint recommends not enthusiasm, not effusion, but "simple" acts, interior tranquility, indifference. The disappropriated soul "no longer violates the laws of indifference in indifferent things"; in a certain way our passions themselves are indifferent things, and the perfect ataraxy could not be indignant about the imperfections imputable to the weakness of our nature. It would simply force itself humbly to destroy them little by little. Saint Francis de Sales especially wished that one avoid "eagerness." The same desire is found in many other French authors of the seventeenth century. The whole doctrine is the exaltation of pure and critical faith, of spiritual tastes and of other apparent signs of fervor. But it was Saint Francis who helped most to see that it was a question of stripping one's own will and of returning it to the will of God alone. To use the image of Dom Mackey in his *Introduction to the Love of God* for the edition of Annecy, the indifferent soul is like the scale in balance which is waiting to tip as soon as one puts something on the scale – the divine will alone determining which side will go up or down. Hence indifference is a state where the soul searches voluntarily to overcome the contradictions of sentiment to the profit of the supernatural; as Saint Francis himself writes: "...the soul that is in this state of indifference and wills nothing but leaves it to God to will what is pleasing to him must be said to have its will in a simple and general state of waiting. To wait is neither to do nor to act, but only to remain subject to some event. If you will examine the matter; this waiting on the part of the soul is truly voluntary. Nevertheless it is not an action but rather a simple disposition to receive whatever shall happen. As soon as the events take place and are received, the waiting changes into consent or acquiescence. But before they occur, the soul is truly in a state of simple waiting, indifferent to all the divine will is pleased to ordain."[55] "To bless God and to thank him for whatever events his providence ordains is truly a holy exercise."[56] Just as the daughter of "the excellent doctor," who confidently let herself be cured without taking her eyes off her father, so our soul must not let its creator out of its sight.

Saint Francis encouraged the virtue of abandon in his religious. He writes in January, 1603: "I beseech you, and also Sister Anne Seguier often to say with the Psalmist: 'I am thine, save me' and with Mary Magdalene kneeling at his feet: 'Rabboni, O my master,' and then leave the rest to him. He will work in you, without your aid, and yet by you and for you and out of you the sanctification of his name, to which be honor and glory."[57] Abandon dispenses from no positive task. There cannot be opposition between the declared will and the will of good pleasure, as we have said: everything sought by the declared will must be fulfilled. True abandon does not exclude prudence but on the contrary demands it. There is a precaution for the health of the body and the soul, which one cannot thoughtlessly abandon because it is manifested by the declared will of God. "Even while we love the abjection which comes of some evil, we must not stop trying to remedy the evil. I shall do what I can not to have a bad sore on my face, but if it comes, I shall love the abjection it brings."[58] If Saint Francis de Sales recommends abandon to Saint Jeanne de Chantal as an "amorous sleeping" of the spirit between the hands of our Lord, without ever ceasing to cooperate carefully with his holy grace by the exercise of virtues and the occasions which present themselves[59] – if he affirms that "a religious who is completely given up into the hands of God...has nothing to do except remain close to Our Lord, without troubling herself about anything, either as regards her body or her soul," at the same time be understands clearly that one must "consider those things for which we are individually responsible." Everything indicates in his development that he wishes to safeguard human activity in its proper place: "So it is with the soul which has surrendered itself; it has nothing else to do but to rest in the arms of our Lord like a child at its mother's breast. When she puts him down to walk, he walks until she takes him up again, and when she wishes to carry him, he allows her to do so. He neither knows nor thinks where he is going, but allows himself to be carried or led wherever his mother pleases. So this soul lets itself be carried when it lovingly accepts God's good pleasure in all things that happen, and walks when it carefully effects all that the known will of God demands."[60]

In effect, abandon does not suppress repugnance and it does not always spare the soul of very difficult interior struggles. Its goal is not to prevent feeling suffering. It resides in the superior part of the soul: desires contrary to the will of God can exist at the same time in the inferior part of the soul. Abandon is one of those "virtues which reside in the higher region of our soul: the lower, generally speaking, has nothing to do with them. We must remain at peace, and paying no attention whatever to what that lower nature desires, we must embrace the divine will and unite ourselves to it whatever this may entail."[61]

It must not be exclusive. Abandon does not replace the other virtues, it must accompany them, it cannot take its place. Alone, it does not suffice. Abandon is important to perfection; but it is not all perfection. However, if this virtue is not exclusive, if, as in the teaching of Saint Francis de Sales, it guarantees the human will its irreplaceable field of action, it is perfectly legitimate. He wrote to a superior of the Visitation: "Ask nothing and refuse nothing whatever in religious life. Holy indifference will keep you at peace with your eternal spouse...."[62] Because it is a source of peace, abandon is a cause of happiness and joy. The act of abandon assures the soul perfect tranquility: "We live in very great security if we give everything to God. We do not confide ourselves to God only in part, and in part to ourselves."[63]

In the same way he recommends as one of the principal preparations for the reception of the sacraments "total abandonment of ourselves to the mercy of God, the submission of our will and all of our affections without reserve to his dominion....Our Lord desiring to give Himself wholly to us, wishes that we on our part, should give ourselves entirely to Him."[64] He who taught this doctrine, lived life fully. This attitude of acceptance, of loving dependence, abandon, was truly the fundamental attitude of soul of Saint Francis de Sales. This indifference is not the atony of the weak and irresolute character who cannot reject anything because he does not know how to choose, who is capable of loving nothing; it is the result of a noble and just appreciation by which not finding anything lovable other than God, the soul esteems only those things which proportionally can aid it to attain its essential end – the glory of its creator – and subsequently its own happiness. But in order that the divine will touch this human will constituted in the state of supernatural indifference, and by this act losing its neutrality, it sets out with all its energy in the direction indicated to it by the movement from on high. This admirable and sanctifying disposition is compatible with the human emotions and feelings, with the contradictions of the inferior part, and it is even in these contradictions that it attains its final perfection.

Saint Francis gives us a marvelous example of this abandon. Love made him conscious that he was entirely in God's hands.

In concluding our study of abandon, we realize that there are other virtues which show that Saint Francis de Sales was not Stoic. Before undertaking a brief synthesis of Salesian spirituality, let us consider his state of soul and mind. He received a humanistic education based on classical studies. In effect, he immersed himself in the classicists, but not to the same degree as so many of his contemporaries. He often cited Aristotle, Plato,

Epictetus, Seneca, Ovid, Martial and many others, but he kept his own independence. These authors are for him tutors rather than his masters. Even as a student he is not content with exposing their doctrine on happiness or the end and duties of man. He corrects them and he completes them by the Christian doctrine.[65] This was characteristic of his spirit; he was very learned, but he was not satisfied in his own knowledge. He rather used what be learned by assimilating and improving it.

Chapter II Endnotes

1   *Initiation theologique*, Paris, Cerf, 1952, II, p. 152.

2   *Oeuvres*, VI, p. 165 [Gasquet, p. 281].

3   *Ibid.*, p. 266 [Gasquet, p. 282].

4   *Ibid.*, V, p. 126 [Ryan, II, p. 111].

5   *Ibid.*, VI, p. 264 [Gasquet, p. 284].

6   *Ibid.*, VI, p. 23 [*Ibid.*, p. 20].

7   *Ibid.*, V, p. 119 [Ryan, II, p. 105].

8   *Ibid.*, VI, p. 270 [Gasquet, p. 286].

9   *Ibid.*, XIII, p. 138.

10   *Ibid.*, V, p. 159 [Ryan, II, p. 136].

11   *Ibid.*, p. 158.

12   *Ibid.*, p. 114 [Ryan, II, p. 100].

13   *Ibid.*, p. 118 [Ryan, II, p. 104].

14   *Ibid.*, VI, pp. 383-89 [Gasquet, pp. 399-406].

15   *Ibid.*, V, pp. 152-55 [Ryan, II, pp. 131-34].

16   *Ibid.*, VI, pp. 31-53 [Gasquet, pp. 29-53].

17   *Ibid.*, VI, pp. 155-60 [Ryan, II, pp. 134-37].

18   Luke, XXII, 42.

19   Matthew, XXVI, 39.

20   *Discourses*, I, 1.

21   *Ibid.*, III, 24.

22   *Oeuvres*, VI, p. 23 [Gasquet, p. 19].

23   *Ibid.*, XII, p. 366.

24   *Ibid.*, V, p. 61 [Ryan, II, p. 59].

25   Serouet, P., *De la vie devoté a la vie mystique*, p. 239.

26   *Ibid.*

27   *Discourses*, III, 37.

28   *Oeuvres*, VI, p. 22 [Gasquet, p. 19].

29   *Ibid.*, VI, p. 384 [Gasquet, p. 400].

30   *Oeuvres*, XVI, p. 133 ff. [Stopp, p. 217].

31   *Ibid.*, VI, p. 23 [Gasquet, p. 19].

32   *Ibid.*, V, p. 122 [Ryan, II, p. 107].

33   *Ibid.*, p. 125 [*Ibid.*, p. 109].

34   *Ibid.*, p. 126 [*Ibid.*, p. 111].

35   *Ibid.*, pp. 137-39 [*Ibid.*, pp. 119-21].

36   *Ibid.*, p. 143 [*Ibid.*, p. 124].

37   *Ibid.*, pp. 146-60 [*Ibid.*, p. 126 ff.].

38   *Ibid.*, p. 147 [*Ibid.*, p. 128].

39   *Ibid.*, p. 148 [*Ibid.*].

40   *Ibid.*, p. 149 [*Ibid.*, p. 129].

41   *Ibid.*, p. 151 [*Ibid.*, p. 130].

42   *Ibid.*, p. 150 ff. [*Ibid.*, pp. 129-30].

43   *Ibid.*, p. 151 [*Ibid.*, p. 130].

44   *Ibid.*, p. 152 ff. [*Ibid.*, p. 131].

45   *Ibid.*, p. 156 [*Ibid.*, p. 134].

46   *Ibid.*

47   *Ibid.*, p. 158 [*Ibid.*, p. 136].

48   *Ibid.*, p. 159 [*Ibid.*, pp. 136-37].

49   *Ibid.*, pp. 160-63 [*Ibid.*, pp. 137-40].

50   *Ibid.*, XVII, pp. 214-20.

40

51   *Ibid.*, p. 79 [Stopp, p. 233].

52   Gore, J.- L., *La Notion d'indifference chez Fenelon et ses sources*, p. 71.

53   Bernières, *Oeuvres*, II.

54   Lavelle, L., *The Meaning of Holiness*, p. 93 ff.

55   *Oeuvres*, V, pp. 158-59 [Ryan, II, p. 136].

56   *Ibid.*, V, p. 155 [*Ibid.*, p. 134].

57   *Ibid.*, XII, p. 170 [Stopp, p. 47].

58   *Ibid.*, XIII, p. 201.

59   *Fragments du petit livre de Ste J. de Chantal*, t. 2, p. 15.

60   *Oeuvres*, VI, p. 27 ff. [Gasquet, p. 24 ff.].

61   *Ibid.*, p. 30 [Gasquet, p. 28].

62   *Ibid.*, XX, p. 298.

63   Saint Augustin, *De dono perseverantiae*, VI.

64   *Oeuvres*, VI, pp. 339-40 [Gasquet, p. 350].

65   *Ibid.*, I, pp. XLI-XLII.

CHAPTER III

The End of Man and Salesian Means

This study will show Saint Francis, as H. Bremond expresses it, "in the school of grace and of souls."[1] He always proceeds step by step, testing each state of spiritual ascension to union with God in which he knows how to unite the ascetic effort with the action of divine grace. The reason for his success is that he does not speak of what he himself would not have tried. Not a single theory, not a single abstract word but what comes from his heart, from his own experience, everywhere he descends to the very roots.[2]

A product of humanism, he surpasses humanism and constructs on it a spiritual edifice. He knows the more precious gifts: faith, grace, supernatural action. The ideal of the Christian, at least for him, is not written on pages but in his heart. It will never change. To forget the supernatural element in his concept of true formation would be to distort his whole spirit: "Although we can read him through profane books, we must always do so in the light of Christian mystics, of which he is one."[3]

In the school of Saint Francis, the end of the Christian life is God. We come from God; we belong to God; we are for God, in view of our eternal salvation: "...he really created angels and men, and to put his providence into effect he furnished and does furnish by his governance all that is needed by rational creatures to attain to glory. Hence, to put it one word, supreme providence is nothing else than the act by which God wills to furnish men and angels the means necessary or useful for attaining their end."[4]

For him, the three great metaphysical proofs of the existence of God, the idea of the infinite being, of the perfect being and of the necessary being, cannot be solidly established except within Christianity. The reason for this is simple: these proofs are valid only in a system which admits of creation. Outside of creation the ideas of the infinite of the perfect and of the necessary are changed: with a coexistent matter the infinite is no longer infinite since the latter is limited by the former; the perfect is no longer perfect, because one would conceive it as more perfect if he had the power to create matter and not only to coordinate it. Finally, the necessary is no longer necessary, since the necessary is necessarily one, and that in the hypothesis, there would be two necessaries. It is the same as if, in place of a preexistent matter, one would admit emanation. If God needs to be developed, there is no longer an infinite, because the infinite is that to which one can add nothing. It is actual. There is no longer anything perfect, since one supposes that its life lacks something which would give it further development in the world; finally, there is no longer anything necessary, or rather everything is necessary because it is the existence of the contingent which makes the distinction of the necessary and, by hypothesis, there is no longer any contingent. That explains why Stoicism, and generally every system which begins with pantheism in a more or less recognized way, has been so poor in its metaphysical speculations on this important question. They lacked a point of departure: namely, the idea of creation.

Let us go on to God's nature. Stoicism is not elevated to the veritable notion of spirituality. It has kept the name without retaining the thing. The spirit, in this philosophy, is not the incorporeal substance, but that which is more subtle, more difficult to identify, that which more possesses the quintessence of the matter; the spirit is invisible ether, the ether diffused throughout the world, which it penetrates with its essence, whose soul it is and which it consequently renders living and divine.

This false notion of spirituality is due to the ideas in the philosophy current at that time, an influence from which Stoicism could not escape although it was a protest against these doctrines. Let us examine this for a moment.

To spirituality, Christianity adds asceticism. God is the necessary and absolute being. *Ego sum qui sum. Qui est misit me ad te.*[5] Christian speculation advances from this point to deduce the resulting divine attributes. If God is the necessary being, he is one, infinite, all powerful, eternal, unchangeable, etc. Furthermore, he possesses all the moral attributes which flow from metaphysical attributes; goodness, wisdom, justice, holiness. However, Stoicism too acknowledges in God most of these attributes. Zeno admitted unity:[6] and Cleanthus, in some verses which Clement of Alexandria has conserved for us, enumerates eternity, omnipotence, immutability, goodness, justice and holiness. Goodness especially was the object of his particular attention. It would be easy here to point out an inconsistency and to put our finger on the basic incompatibility that there is between a material substance and such attributes.

As for Providence, it is to Stoicism's honor to have proclaimed it on high. Chrysippus and Seneca had written a book on Providence. It was assuredly a salutary and social thought to insist on this dogma at a time when skepticism was invading souls and when the learned classes of society scarcely any longer accepted the idea of divine intervention in human activities. Unfortunately, in Stoic theory, Providence does not conserve its true character. The primitive Stoics and Seneca himself scarcely saw anything in it except the constancy of the laws of nature.[7] Stoicism, as we have seen, brings about the descent of the supreme cause from the metaphysical to the physical and then it becomes "destiny"; destiny subjecting everything, and subjected itself to necessity. Nevertheless the destiny of the Stoics is not a brute and blind force. If it is the cause of everything, then it is the seminal reason which contains all particular reasons. It is the idea that everything is foreseen and determined beforehand, it is the universal providence[8] God and nature are only one, it is from God himself that the economy of the world flows.[9]

But that does not mean that God governs the world in such a way as human wisdom would – by abstract ideas, and as an object exterior to himself – no, this is by a concrete art, interior to his works and which is only the tendency of which they are the form and the immediate expression. This art is for the Stoics the divine art. The seminal reasons for which God predetermines and does everything are hence so many states through which he passes, so many forms in which he clothes himself. It is God himself who penetrates and circulates everywhere, as honey in the honeycomb. It is God himself who, without form by himself, is transformed into everything, and makes himself all to all.[10]

We have seen that there is in the Christian idea of creation this first relation of cause to effect.[11] Thus there exists between heaven and the Christian virtues a direct relationship, because virtue is the unique "paradise here below" according to the word of our holy doctor.[12] Between the idea of virtue and recompense there is a direct relationship, as well as between the idea of vice and punishment.

Stoicism[13] and Christianity respectively admitted this doctrine. But there is a point on which they are separated by a profound difference: it is that of knowing if merit and demerit are susceptible of more or less, and if they vary according to the actions of the agent. Stoicism takes as its point of departure this principle that conformity or disagreement with reason is the unique measure of good and bad, and that there are no degrees in this conformity and this disagreement because they are or are not. Hence one concludes that all virtues are equal as well as all vices, and consequently that all good actions and all evil actions are a participation in vice and virtue.

Reason equals reason, as a straight line equals a straight line; hence, virtue is equal to virtue, since it is nothing other than right reason. All virtues are right reasons; such as is reason, such are the actions. They are all equals; if they are right, they are equal; because being like to reason, they are also like between themselves. All virtues are equal, all virtuous acts and all men who produce them.[14]

Christianity and common sense reject this doctrine. We say everyday: this man is more virtuous than another, this action is less good than that one. All of humanity speaks this language, and this language is that of common sense. To give alms to a poor man when one is a millionaire, or to contribute a penny taken out of bread money, are two good actions; who will maintain that the merit is the same in both cases? To tell the truth when it costs nothing, and to die for the truth, are two good acts; who has ever pretended outside of the systems that the two acts are equal? If the Stoic theory happened to prevail, the level of morality would soon be lowered. What good does it do to seek the perfection of good when the good is sufficient? Or rather, the good, by the fact that it is good, is all perfection, since it has no degrees: emulation disappears, and the idea of progress, so deeply engraved in the human conscience, is no longer anything except a word empty of sense. But Stoicism takes it upon itself to reverse its theory. After having begun with the principle that virtue being perfection, can neither grow nor diminish, that it cannot be more or less strained or relaxed, because it is like a ruler, like a straight line, that is, to the highest degree of tension which is possible (Seneca: Letter LXXI); that virtue is wisdom itself or it is nothing, that there is no middle point between wisdom and folly, so it is between the straight line and the curved (Seneca: Letter LXXIV); he is obliged to arrive at this conclusion, that all good and right actions are equal, because these are only different applications of one and the same principle, which does not know any degrees; that all bad actions are likewise equal; and consequently, that all virtuous men are wise, and that all wise men are perfectly wise; that all those who are not, are completely foolish, vicious and miserable; and that, finally, whoever has a virtue has all the virtues, and whoever has a vice has all the other vices, and the one or the other to the highest degree. Now, after these extravagant conclusions, who is not surprised to hear Stoicism teach that the proper things, accomplished in view of order and beauty by the wise man, from right actions, and by the constant exercise of all these acts, without omitting any one of them, constitute a common virtue and wisdom, imperfect resemblance without doubt of virtue and of absolute wisdom, but which serves however to lead one to it. These assertions, as we see, so sufficiently refute themselves that we do not feel the need to insist thereupon.

Such is the necessity, such also is the charm of the Christian virtues which Saint Francis de Sales traces for us in a magnificent picture. We should like to establish the principal traits of Salesian spirituality in order to help replace in their vital context the diverse elements of the thought of the Saint. We shall see by this spiritual synthesis that Salesian virtue had nothing to do with "Stoic virtue."

The following are some elements of Salesian spirituality: 1) primacy of love; 2) imitation of Jesus Christ; 3) docility to the holy spirit; 4) sense of the Church; 5) asceticism orientated toward the flowering of mystical graces; 6) prayer; 7) mysticism and symbolism of spiritual childhood, by which Saint Francis is pleased to present the flowering in love.

We have already seen in Chapter II that love holds a prime place in the thought of Saint Francis. From where has this idea come? His family education, the strong Franciscan influences which were present during his youth, teaching received from his teachers and Jesuit directors, the influence of the *Spiritual Combat*, the work of Saint Theresa, controversy in the Chablais with the Calvinist ministers, and finally the natural leaning of his own sentiment all lead him to discover in God the visage of love. The temptation to despair in 1586 was only an episode. That terrible confrontation of Francis with the justice of God will anchor forever in his being the conviction that God is a God of love. "God is love." And the union of the soul with God is brought about in and by love. If, in Book Five of the *Treatise*, Francis de Sales analyzes the difference between the love of complacence and the love of benevolence, and his analyses are precious, then he would recall to us that it is more important to love than to reason: "The perfection of the Christian life consists in the conformity of our will with that of our God." [15]

This conviction concerning the primacy of love perhaps made him slightly underestimate speculative mysticism. He will accent much more the love of God than the light of God. To the Dionysian ecstacy of understanding, Francis de Sales will prefer the ecstacy of the will, and still more the ecstacy of life, which, without extraordinary manifestations, only produces a soul empty of itself and no longer living except in the life itself of God.

Henry Bremond has done justice to certain strange allegations which would make of Francis de Sales a "deist or shameful Christian." [16] If Salesian doctrine does not insist as much as one might hope on our incorporation with Christ by baptism, it does give a very important place to Our Lord's humanity: "The most ordinary abode of the soul ought to be near the cross, and the daily bread of religion ought to be the meditation of the passion." [17]

In manus tuas, Domine, commendo spiritum meum "is the essential word of love; it is the soul of love."[18]

The imitation of Jesus Christ surpasses our strength. This is why Francis recommends that one permit himself to be formed interiorly by the spirit of Jesus. It is to the gift of piety that he especially attributes the birth of the filial spirit: "O gift of piety, rich present that God makes to the heart. Happy is he who possesses this correspondence of the filial heart toward the paternal heart of the celestial father."[19] In his *Treatise*, Francis exposes his original concept of the gifts of the holy spirit; for him, the the gifts "are not only inseparable from charity, but they are the principal virtues, properties and qualities of charity."[20] A "devout" soul is a soul totally docile to the holy spirit. Furthermore, at this summit, everything is joined together again: filial love, perfect conformity with Jesus Christ, perfect indifference and total abandon.

The Church is not for Francis de Sales the prize for a combat, but a source of life. In restoring Christian life to the interior of the church for which he had become the pastor, he worked efficaciously to restore to the body of Christ its visible unity. The "doctor of devotion," of "individual perfection," has not failed to recognize the mystical reality of the Church. If he does not employ the expression "Mystical Body" he does know the reality and he lives with it.

This love is given to us in and by the Church: "All the doctrine that she proclaims consists of sacred love. This love is of a red more brilliant than scarlet because it is inflamed by the blood of her spouse, and it is sweeter than honey because of the sweetness of the Beloved who covers her over with delights."[21] This is the teaching of the Church that he intends to expose. In effect, "In holy Church all is by love, in love, for love, and of love."[22] About this he says: "The things I have set forth are not so much those I learned in earlier days of disputation, but rather those which concern for the service of souls and twenty-four years spent in sacred preaching lead me to think are most conducive to the glory of the Gospel and of the Church."[23] The redemptive death of Christ inspires in him analogous reflections. Jesus "gave himself up to the very last drop of his blood in order to make a sacred cement with which he wished to bind, to join, to attach every stone of his Church, which are the faithful."[24]

A spirituality centered on love is expressed concretely by the search for the will of God, conformity inspired by a ceaseless love pure in its desire and the "death" of one's own will realized in holy indifference and abandon.

Like his master Saint Ignatius at the beginning of the *Spiritual Exercises*, Francis strives to convince his disciple that "man is created in order to praise, venerate and serve God." All the rest is means. From the point of departure, asceticism is thus deliberately oriented toward the summits. To the sinner who hesitates, he shows immediately the flowering of love to which God calls him: "the soul that aspires to the honor of being the spouse of the Son of God must put off the old man, and put on the new, by forsaking sin."[25] Love is the alpha and the omega of Salesian spirituality. Francis de Sales never envisages the work of purification, of stripping of oneself, uniquely under its purely human aspect, but as a progressive invasion of love. The virtues themselves are modalities of charity.

The great obstacle to the love of God is self love. "Self love never dies until we ourselves die; it has thousands of ways of entrenching itself in our soul, but we cannot cast it out."[26]

In the acquisition of virtues, one must keep in mind the direction of the goal toward which they ought to help us, which is the perfection of charity. Francis de Sales rightly recommends the virtues which are in more direct relationship with charity. Humility "makes us love our own abjection," it is directly opposed to self love – on condition that it does not concern a disguised seeking for the esteem of others: "We often say that we are nothing, that we are misery itself and the refuse of the world; but we should be very sorry if anyone should take us at our word or tell others that we are really such miserable wretches as we say."[27] When one knows the Salesian concept of perfection and humility, it is not difficult to find the most profound reason for which St Francis de Sales has placed humility as the basis of our spiritual life: it is that which performs the work – necessary and indispensable – setting aside all obstacles to the reception of the gift of God; grace in giving to God the possibility of acting by charity. "To receive the grace of God into our hearts," says the holy doctor, "they must be emptied of our own vainglory."[28]

Francis de Sales recommends the virtues which best infuse fraternal charity into daily life, namely patience and meekness. Meekness, according to St. Francis de Sales, is so important that, without it, true fraternal charity is nearly impossible. "The balm, which, as I have before observed, always sinks beneath all other liquors, represents humility. The olive oil, which always rises to the top, represents meekness and mildness, which surmount all things and excel amongst virtues, as being the flower of charity. This...is in its perfection when it is not only patient but meek and mild."[29] On the contrary, he who is mild not only possesses the opposed virtues, but also the incomparable strength which draws others, because mildness, that "cream of charity"[30] is the most captivating of all the virtues and the most capable of winning souls.

It seems remarkable here that mildness is related inseparably to the name and even the physiognomy of St. Francis de Sales. "Mildness," writes Hamon, "seems to sum up the whole life of St. Francis de Sales: it is this virtue that the faithful have emulated as his distinctive feature. If he has done great things, it is especially due to the influence of his mildness; if he converted many sinners and heretics, raised to perfection so many just souls, consoled so many afflicted hearts, it is by the unction of his mildness. Finally if the books he wrote have produced and still produce every day so much fruit in the Church, it is because his mildness is shown on every page and seems itself to have written every line."[31]

We cannot find a better resume of all that we have said on the gracious condescension and mildness of St. Francis de Sales than in the confidence that he showed to Mother de Chantal in a letter from the year 1620 to 1621. We find there how all that is blended with the love of God, is, in effect, the consequence and the expression of that love of God. The following shows us that his life and his doctrine were one and the same. "There is no soul in the world, at least to my way of thinking, who cherishes more cordially, tenderly and, to say it once and for all, more amorously than I; because it was pleasing to God to make my heart in this way...: but it is marvelous how I can accommodate all that together, because it is my opinion that I never love anything other than God and all souls for God."[32]

Mildness and the Christian method of Salesian virtues have given us this *saint* Francis and many others as well. Could Stoicism be compared with this Salesian system? If one objects that the vices of those who profess a doctrine prove nothing against its principles, that from the fact that there have been bad Stoics, one cannot conclude that Stoicism is bad; no more than one could conclude that Christianity is bad because there are bad Christians. But what can one say, nevertheless, of a doctrine which has been sterile to the point of not having produced a single truly virtuous man, or even simply a man who lived in conformity with its principles? Because this is the reproach that Epictetus addressed to the Stoics of his time, the confession is significant: "Show him: I desire, by the gods, to see a Stoic. You cannot show me one fashioned so; but show me at least one who is forming, who has shown a tendency to be a Stoic. Do me this favour: do not grudge(sic) an old man seeing a sight which I have not yet seen."[33] This statement is perfectly clear.

In concluding these considerations, if we wish to grasp all the importance that St. Francis de Sales attaches to mildness, it is essential to recall that, for him, charity necessarily demands humility and that mildness is only a special form taken by humility when it is a question of loving our neighbour. In one of his sermons, he states very clearly his first and fundamental value of humility: "Humility is so necessary to us that without it we cannot be agreeable to God or have any other virtue, not even charity which perfects all, because it is so joined to humility that these two virtues cannot be separated."[34]

Thus the terms humility and mildness only indicate one and the same virtue according to the way the latter is used in the love of God or in the love of neighbour. The two words are synonymous and they would be practically interchangeable if St. Francis de Sales were not worried about being misunderstood. Perhaps it would also be well to underline a nuance which has some importance. Humility, in recalling to us our nothingness, better characterizes our attitude toward God, while mildness defines more clearly, more essentially our relations with our neighbour.

These are the essential elements of Salesian asceticism, each oriented toward the flowering of love. There is no absolute predicting from the timid love of beginners to the love which embraces the heart of the saints. Without speaking to Philothea about the summits he desires for her, Francis nevertheless knows that the way that he points out must, by the pure mercy of God, lead her there one day. It is from this point of view that we must consider the other points of Salesian asceticism. It is sufficient to recall here what constitutes the profound unity of it all.

There are no little Salesian "occupations"; all the exercises prescribed to Philothea are, from the very beginning, oriented toward consummation in love.

The ejaculatory prayers are said "to give you a love of God and to arouse yourself to a passionate and tender affection for this divine Spouse."[35] "If out of love for God the soul seeks a way to be freed from her troubles, she will seek it with patience, meekness, humility and tranquility."[36] "The slightest mortifications which present themselves independently of ourselves are the best and ought to be preferred to the greatest performed of our own choice...where there is less of our own choice, there is more of God's will."[37]

Hence it is always a very clear awareness of the goal to be attained which guides St. Francis de Sales in implementing ways of perfection.

Francis takes great care not to consider mental prayer as a panacea. Although he gave Philothea a method of mental prayer, he knew that "real love has no set method."[38] Prayer is worth what love is worth where it is deeply rooted, and it is by its fruits that we must judge it. What the saint demands of his penitents, is that they be habitually turned toward God; hence this constant orientation of their life will flower, every time that their state of life permits them the leisure, in formal acts of prayer.

The consciousness of the divine presence is the first point in the method of mental prayer that Francis recommends to beginners. Francis will make known, if he has not created it, the term "prayer of simple presence" to designate what St. Theresa calls a "prayer of recollection" or of "quietude," thus underlining the cause which produces it as opposed to the effect. "Therefore, my dear daughters, you will be praying well if you keep yourselves in peace and tranquility close to Our Lord, or at least in His sight, with no other desire or intention than to be with Him, and to content Him."[39] The prayer of simple presence consists in being present to God, not in meditating on His presence or feeling it; in this quietude, "the will acts solely by a most simple acquiescence in God's good pleasure, since it wills to be in prayer without any aim but to be in God's sight as it shall please him."[40] This last text makes very clear that it is a question of loving presence, even if perfectly incomprehensible to us: "O true God! how good is this way of keeping in God's presence so as to be and to wish always and forever to be at his good pleasure! Thus, so I believe in all conditions, yes, even in profound sleep we are still more profoundly in God's most holy presence."[41] When the soul emerges from the night, the feeling of the presence is returned to him with an exceptional purity and intensity, but of that St. Francis scarcely speaks. He speaks, on the contrary, of the highest degree of placing ourselves before God which corresponds with the keenest realization of his presence. This is total abandon, the summit of holy indifference.

St. Francis de Sales knows that God calls all men to perfection since he gave them a commandment to tend toward it; he knows that this perfection is the perfection of love, and that of its nature "divine love is ecstatic, since it does not permit lovers to live for themselves, but rather for the thing beloved."[42] When the soul engages the ascetic means taught to Philothea in order not to live for itself, God ordinarily performs what it cannot do even with the collaboration of ordinary grace, without which nothing can be done. And by new means, which mark its entry into the mystical life, God produces this stripping, this purifiation, this emptiness which will permit love to expand. The roots of sin are sunk to a depth at which the soul cannot act, because there its conscious activity does not have access. Not that it be henceforth passive under the action of God, but what God expects from it is not more initiative, but rather acquiescence.

The mystical life is simultaneously a death to self and a life in Jesus Christ. According to their particular grace, certain mystical writers have insisted on the aspect of death and others on that of life, or, in more poetic terms, on the luminous or nocturnal aspect of mystical experience. Francis de Sales, in Books Six and Seven of the *Treatise*, since he was then using St. Theresa as his principle guide, presents the mystical development of the soul under the aspect of progress made in light and in love. But in Book Nine, speaking especially in the light of the experience of Jeanne de Chantal who was guided by some very profound sights, he uses another vocabulary. One wonders sometimes where he would introduce holy abandon or holy indifference in the Theresian itinerary. Vain preoccupation. "Very holy indifference," neither precedes nor follows "union": it is the same thing, seen from a diametrically opposed angle.

Without returning to the Salesian mystical ladder, it is remarkable that in speaking of "exercises of holy love in mental prayer" Francis was very naturally led to present preferably the positive and luminous aspects of mystical experience. But be realized this was not the whole experience, since he could not include that of Jeanne de Chantal. We already notice in Book Seven, through the distinction between the sentiment of union and habitual union "at the summit and supreme point of the spirit," that Francis de Sales doe not wish to reserve the name of union to the luminous aspects of the prayer of union. In fact, he again treats of union in Book Nine, a book consecrated to holy indifference and which he entitles: "Concerning the love of submission by which our will is united to the good pleasure of God." If Salesian indifference has sometimes been considered as a totally passive disposition, as a non-willing, it is due to the fact that something apparently essential was forgotten: indifference is not the whole, but rather the nocturnal aspect of love.

Salesian spirituality is centered on the abandon of the soul into the hands of God. Francis de Sales willingly compares this abandon to the attitude of the little child in his mother's arms, an image which he borrows from the great Castilian mystic.[43] But Theresa of Avila does not exaggerate the comparison; her love for the Lord was a wife's love and she stresses this fidelity and intimacy; the summit of her spiritual ascension is a "marriage." But it is completely different for Francis de Sales and we must place him in the long series of spiritual writers who, before St. Theresa of the Child Jesus, presented the intimacy of the soul with its God under the aspect of spiritual childhood.

So, to recapitulate a little, Stoicism, whose point of departure is in pantheism, places itself in the radically impossible position of being anything other than a moral parody. Since God himself is the principle of man's acts, vice as well as error become impossible, and consequently virtue is abolished. St. Francis, on the contrary, begins with creation and retains virtue as a proper object.

Stoicism, with the pretention of founding a spiritual moral, produces the most materialistic moral possible: because it proposes to man no other goal than the conservation and the development of his constitution. In Christianity, the goal that man proposes to attain is placed higher than the organism, and consequently his moral is truly spiritual.

According to Stoicism, there is only one virtue for which all acts are equal as well as for all acts of vice. According to St. Francis de Sales, there are several virtues differentiated by their object, and several degrees of virtues measured according to the habit and the intensity of the acts.

The Stoics teach that virtue is inadmissible; Christians profess that it can be lost or altered, and that it can be lost no matter what degree might have been attained.

Stoicism proposes to man the accomplishment of duty by the motivation of duty. He presents to his thought only an abstraction which is powerless, especially at the hour of passion, to retain the will in good. St. Francis, in placing before his eyes God himself as the ultimate reason for duty, enlivens his imagination by this concrete idea, and determines his will to conform to that of the master.

The Stoic moral, in prescribing the accomplishment of duty by the unique motive of duty and in eliminating as impure every motive of personal interest, even the superior, offers man so elevated an ideal that his weakness does not permit him to attain it. The Christian morale in joining to the motive of duty that of recompense in a world where every act of conscience will produce its last effect, proposes to us a motive more proportioned to our weakness, and proves, at the same time, a more profound and more exact metaphysical knowledge in not separating the sovereign happiness from the sovereign good.

This sovereign good itself, during so long a time and so vainly sought by ancient philosophy, is placed by Stoicism in the life perfectly conformed to nature and to reason, producing the harmony of the natural faculties, and bordering finally on ataraxy, that is, on insensibility; while Christianity, with the high and sovereign reason which characterizes it, surpasses the frontiers of the sensible world after having upset the whole scaffolding of these childish solutions, is going to place this sovereign good in the being who as the source of others must also be their end, and who, forever satisfying their every legitimate aspiration, constitutes for every soul the sovereign good by its possession.

Stoicism, having offered us from its wisdom a sublime ideal, feeling that it is above human strength, declares it unrealizable, and destroys by the act the whole moral edifice so laboriously constructed. St. Francis de Sales, on the contrary, shows us the true type of perfection in a way which is proper to simple creatures; to each man, according to his capacity, he shows God.

Such are the profound and radical differences which separate the Salesian moral from the Stoic moral. How then can we claim that St. Francis de Sales could have been a Stoic?

Chapter III Endnotes

1   Bremond, H., *Sainte Chantal*, p. 112.

2   *Oeuvres*, IV, p. 9 [Ryan, I, p. 41].

3   Liuima, A., *op. cit.*, I, p. 152.

4   *Oeuvres*, IV, p. 96 [Ryan, I, pp. 108-09].

5   Exod., III, 14.

6   Diogenes Laertius, *The Life of Zeno*.

7   *The Treatise on Providence*.

8   Plutarch, *De communibus notius versus Stoicos*, 36.

9   Plutarch, *De stoicorum repugnantis*, 34.

10   Tertullian, *De anima*.

11   *Vide supra*, III, p. 68.

12   *Oeuvres*, III, p. 169.

13   Seneca, Letter XV.

14   Seneca, Letter LXVI.

15   *Oeuvres*, XXVI, p. 185.

16   *Op. cit.*, III, p. 47 [III, p. 38].

17   *Oeuvres*, XXI, p. 158.

18   *Ibid.*, V, p. 477.

19   *Ibid.*, X, p. 423.

20   *Ibid.*,V, p. 292 [Ryan, II, p. 240].

21   *Ibid.*, IV, p. 3 [Ryan, I, p. 37].

22   *Ibid.*, p. 4 [*Ibid.*, p. 38].

23   *Ibid.*, p. 13 ff. [*Ibid.*, p. 44].

24   *Ibid.*, X, p. 277.

25   *Ibid.*, III, p. 26 [Ryan, I, p. 43].

26   *Ibid.*, XII, p. 383 [Stopp, p. 77].

27   *Ibid.*, III, p. 147 [Ryan, I, p. 131].

28   *Ibid.*, p. 139 [*Ibid.*, p. 128].

29   *Ibid.*, p. 161 [*Ibid.*, p. 141].

30   *Ibid.*, IX, p. 283.

31   *Ibid.*, II, p. 506.

32   *Ibid*, XX, p. 216.

33   *Discourses*, II, 19.

34   *Oeuvres*, t. 9, p. 224.

35   *Ibid.*, III, p. 95 [Ryan, p. 94].

36   *Ibid.*, p. 311 [*Ibid.*, p. 254].

37   *Processus remissorialis gebennenis*, I, 28.

38   *Oeuvres*, XVIII, p. 239 [Stopp, p. 159].

39   *Ibid.*, VI, p. 349 [Gasquet, p. 360].

40   *Ibid.*, IV, p. 342 [Ryan, I, p. 299].

41   *Ibid.*, p. 342 [*Ibid.*, p. 298 ff.].

42   *Ibid.*, V, p. 24 [Ryan, II, p. 28].

43   *Ibid.*, IV, p. 334 [Ryan, I, p. 292].

CONCLUSION

Stoic works influenced St. Francis de Sales, although he was not a Stoic.

The profound reason then for the differences and oppositions in the ancients is the absence of the theological virtue which establishes and includes all the others in Salesian spirituality, namely, charity. In them "repentance of this kind is joined to that knowledge of love of God which nature can furnish; it is a result of moral religion. Natural reason has given more knowledge than love to philosophers, for they have not glorified God in proportion to their knowledge of him. So also nature has furnished more light to understand how God is offended by sin than ardor to arouse the repentance required to repair the offense."[1]

Stoicism then lacks love: love of God who is too little known, love of others, transitory individuals and even strangers. Also Stoicism brings the reproach of pride, cruelty and deception. Its distortion consists not only in not agreeing in theory and practice, but in recommending condescension and scorn toward human imbecility. To cry with those who cry, to express our sorrow – words – yes. But to permit really shared suffering the access of his soul – no. Francis de Sales does not cite the thought seventeen in the *Manual*, but we know enough about him that his forthright civility and his boundless friendship condemned social pretences as well as affectations of false piety. The true and naively manifested afflictions, direct or indirect effects of love that man has for himself and for his neighbour, find their explanations and at the same time their limits as well as their consolation in the love that he has for God. The badly directed practice of the Stoics, which is not inspired by love but by pride, fails to acknowledge the hierarchy of duties and authorizes the criminal act in order to obtain glory. The *Treatise* in chapter ten of Book Eleven – although it extends its remarks to all "pagans" – cites principally the Stoics, and, following St. Augustine, protests vehemently against the traditional glorification of the heroes of antiquity, revived by the humanism of the sixteenth century and which will be perpetuated by this teaching.

"The one among the Stoics and captains who killed himself in the city of Utica in order to escape a calamity which he estimated unworthy of his life, has been so praised by these profane minds, brought about this action with so little true virtue, that, as St. Augustine says, he did not exhibit courage to avoid dishonesty but a sick soul which is not reassuring when expecting adversity...." He killed himself "because he begrudged Caesar the glory he would gain by granting him his life or because he feared the shame of living under a conqueror whom he hated. For this he may be praised as having crude and perhaps even great courage, but not as having a wise, virtuous and constant soul."[2] He adds this general maxim which is always good to meditate: "Cruelty which is practiced without emotion and in cold blood is the most cruel of all, and it is the same of despair, because that which is the slowest, the most deliberate, the most resolved, is also the least excusable and the most despaired."

The Augustinian interpretation with which St. Francis de Sales agrees causes him to be more severe in his judgment of pagan virtues; "In fact, if the pagans have practiced certain virtues, it has been largely for the sake of worldly glory, and as a result they have had only the bare act of virtue and not the motive and intention. Virtue is not true virtue if it lacks a true intention...." "It was not love of honest virtue, but love of honor that drove on those worldly wise men in the practice of virtue. So too their virtues were as different from true virtue as honor is from honesty and love of merit from love of reward...." "Our ancient Fathers said that the virtues of the pagans were at one and the same time both virtues and non-virtues: virtues because they had luster and show, non-virtues not only because they lacked the vital heat of love of God which alone could make them perfect, but also because they were incapable of receiving such love because they were in persons without faith."[3]

Comparisons increase the severity of these judgments: pagan virtues resemble glow worms which shine in the darkness, not in the clarity of revelation; or rather they are comparable to wormy apples which have color – a little substance, but "the worm of vanity is in the center, which spoils them." With the strength of courage of Caton of Utica or of a Seneca who takes his life for "the vanity of glory," he opposes the invincible courage of the martyrs dying for the glory of truth. He is surprised that admiration accrues to the first, not the second, "a hundred times more worthy of admiration and alone worthy of imitation."

Here Epictetus is not named: we must recall that St. Francis considered him converted "at the moment of death." His conversion, reasonably contested by history, in consequence of the principles professed here, would have made him a part of the too much admired group "of the virtuous non-virtuous."

The "theology" of the Stoics is indecisive and unstable Their "anthropology" and their physiology are improvised and abusively optimistic.[4] Consequently they cannot pretend to regulate human conduct correctly. They have not known nor recognized the unity in the transcendance of God, nor His love, nor the necessity of meditation, alone truly liberating. Their minimum of piety is directed toward an unknown divinity. Hence they risk offending him and not having any consideration except for their own person. Their God or their gods: laws of nature or of destiny, infrangible necessity, do not at all prefigure the unique God, pure spirit, creating power who, out of love for his creature in the irreversible course of history, takes on body and blood.[5] Man, such as they conceive of him, capable of "possessing himself," of being in agreement with himself and with the cosmos, is the sole artisan of his "salvation" or of his happiness. This humanism which tends to eliminate the drama of our condition appears to St. Frances de Sales as a lure. By vocation his view is fixed on Christ; by experience – his and that of others who have confidence in him – he knows that man is painfully and rarely pacified.

Apatheia or ataraxia – indifference impassibility in its full sense – is, in the eyes of Francis de Sales, a chimera or a lie. It is not true that man remains invulnerable in the vicissitudes of existence – as a rock undisturbed by the waves. His nature divided or torn, he is always his own adversary and the intimate drama is never bared definitively here below. In order to find peace, "holy tranquility," he must descend below the surface agitations to the sanctified regions of the soul. Undoubtedly the bishop teaches his religious that virtue is not so terrible a thing as one might imagine it;[6] they are better preserved than the people of the world. But even to that end he does not indicate the flowery ways which agreeably lead to the mastery of self or to full satisfaction. The spiritual combat is not a decorative metaphor used as the title of a book. It is a proper expression for the pathetic signification he has experienced.

Hence *apatheia*, is neither insensibility nor still less impeccability. It is simply domination over sensible impressions become habitual in the believing soul which has thus "mortified its members which are on earth," according to the passage from St. Paul, in order to regenerate its attraction for the things of God. Henceforth it is no longer his emancipated desires which reign, subjected to the impressions of the flesh and the world, but rather the spirit of God. The adherence to *apatheia* has hence as an immediate counterpart the diffusion in our heart of the love of God, of this celestial agape that the holy spirit spreads there by his coming

In the description that they give of this state to which the purgation of the soul is destined by the mortification of the senses, the Fathers draw largely on the teaching of the Stoics. The latter, in effect, already under the name of *apatheia*, teach their wise ideal of a mastery of oneself brought about by the voluntary subjection of the reason to the master of the universe, to the scorn of sensible impressions. However, the Christian *apatheia* differs from the Stoic apathy first in what it is; that is, not simply an acceptance of the impersonal law which rules the whole universe, but an acceptance of the will of a free and all-loving God known by faith. Yet this God leads us there, not by the constraint of his omnipotence to which we can only be passively resigned, but, by the condescendence of his grace. We adhere to the latter, not only freely, but in an act of faith vivified by love which is like the restoration itself of our free will after its having been captive under the yoke of sin, of flesh, the world, and the devil. We can even say, along with St. Paul, that this is a victory of love over the love of God itself, in the sense that the *apatheia* makes us not limit ourselves to a law imposed from the outside, as a constraint on our will, but rather to adhere by the freest filial love possible to generosity, to a creating spontaneity of paternal love.

We have shown[7] that Salesian indifference is not only the ascetic effort by which a soul imposes silence to the preferences of nature, in order to discover, thanks to the "equilibrium of balance," the choice of God. It is true that St. Francis de Sales sometimes uses the word in this sense[8] but ordinarily, indifference for him is the summit of love, which is attained, after the "trespass of the will," by the soul which, perfectly resembling Jesus, according to the measure of grace which is given to it, living in and for him, rejoins him, as if on the cross in the blackest of night, to the summit of total abandon. That is what Francis, insisting here on "death to oneself" which every life in Jesus Christ entails, calls "the ecstacy of life."[9]

We mutually admit the basic opposition of Stoic and Christian doctrine and of the conclusions which they respectively imply. Ravaisson, who had historical information which the Bishop of Geneva did not have and which, furthermore, was foreign to the latter's pastoral and apologetic preoccupations, wrote in the middle of the nineteenth century: "The Christian is as humble as is the Stoic proud. The Christian awaits everything from God who changes hearts; the Stoic awaits nothing except from himself."[10] The antithesis where the subjects are employed, certainly in their ideal signification, does not place false windows on the edifice of the historical thought. It expresses without doubt a general truth that one will not alter. However, erudite curiosity is not forbidden which searches particular truths in an effort to discover within the unity of a school the diversity of personalities. It is so much more authorized than the school (in the wide sense) which has existed longer in varying circumstances and surroundings. It is still possible that an analysis conducted according to the spirit of modern psychology produce somewhat of a reduction among those opposed to delving the regions of obscure motivations, of confused desires which are badly known and badly fulfilled. Thus it is that such an analysis would interpret the heroic scorn of suffering and death among the Stoics as "a hopeless faith in the value of sacrifice."[11] Ravaisson pronounced only the adjective without a modifier and noticed that pride led them to "sadness only a heartbeat from despair."[12]

Whatever these analyses might produce, we do not risk any error in supposing that Francis de Sales would have approved them and that he would have appreciated their positive results.

And furthermore, if he took pleasure in reading the proposals and utterances of Epictetus, it is because his soul profited from it. The interior life, with discernment, without dilettantism, slakes its thirst at many sources.

As Father Liuima, S. J. wrote us in a letter from Rome on the thirteenth of January, 1963:

> How pitiful are the Stoics in face of such a strength of soul. It seems to me in reading the first part of my book *Aux sources du traite de l'amour de Dieu de Saint François de Sales*, where I studied the development of his interior life, you will easily be able to find the sources, or at least the trail to follow in research on sources for his idea of indifference. It is possible that next, after having received it from the Jesuits during his whole life and enriching it by the influence of spiritual authors, he used some images and comparisons for it drawn from pagan authors in order to express himself.

We have seen that there are between the doctrine of the Stoics and that of St. Francis de Sales some very radical and pronounced differences, so pronounced that one is precisely the opposite of the other. That is what we have established in the course of this work. But who can better defend himself than our great saint himself? The Bishop of Belley one day in the company of St. Francis praised the philosophy of Seneca, and alleged that the latter's maxims were very close to those of the Gospel: "Yes, Francis replied, as to the letter, but not at all according to the spirit. – Why that, asked his interlocutor? – Because the spirit of the Gospel aims only at stripping us of ourselves in order to put on Jesus Christ and virtue, to renounce ourselves in order to depend entirely on grace; whereas that philosopher always recalls us to ourselves, he does not at all wish that his wise man share his happiness nor his felicity outside of himself, which is manifestly pride and a very great fault.

The wise Christian must be little in his own eyes, and so little as to consider himself nothing; whereas Seneca wants his wise man to be above all things and esteem himself master of the whole universe and the maker of his own fortune, which is intolerable conceit."[13]   Hence, on the testimony of St. Francis de Sales, the two morals are profoundly different in spirit.

Conclusion Endnotes

1   *Ibid.*, IV, p. 148 [Ryan, I, p. 150 ff.].

2   *Ibid.*, V, p. 271 [Ryan, II, p. 223].

3   *Ibid.*, pp. 272-74 [*Ibid.*, p. 225 ff.].

4   Lagrange, J. M., in *Revue Biblique*, 1921, p. 12.

5   Brehier, A., *Histoire de la Philosophie*, p. 496.

6   *Oeuvres*, IV, p. 124 [Ryan, I, p. 131].

7   *Vide supra*, Ch. I.

8   *Oeuvres*, VI, p. 369 [Gasquet, p. 383].

9   *Ibid.*, V, p. 31 [Ryan, II, p. 33].

10   De Chardin, Teilhard, *The Divine Milieu*, p. 98.

11   Busson, L., *La religion des Classiques*, Paris, 1948, p. 204.

12   *Essai*, II, p. 291.

13   Camus, J. P., *L'esprit du B. François de Sales*, IV, 15 .

BIBLIOGRAPHY

I. SOURCES

Saint Francis de Sales. *Oeuvres.* Edition complete, publié par Dom B. Mackey. Annecy: Nierat, 1892-1963, 27 vol.

II. WORKS

1. *General*

Blanc, Elie. *Dictionnaire de philosophie.* Paris: Lethiel-lieux, 1906, 1247 pp.

Bouyer, Louis. *Introduction a la vie spirituelle.* Paris: Desclee, 1960, 320 pp.

Brasier, V., Morganti, E., St. Durica, M. *Bibliografia Salesiana, Opere et scritti riguardanti San Francesco di Sales (1623-1955).* Torino: Societa Editrice Internazionale, 1956, 104 pp.

Brehier, Emile. *Histoire de la philosophie.* Paris: P.U.F., 1948, 3 vol.

Cognet, Louis. *Post-Reformation Spirituality.* New York: Hawthorne, 1959, 143 pp.

D'Ales, A. *Dictionnaire apologetique de la foi catholique.* Paris: Beauchesne, 1922, 4 vol.

Fouillee, Alfred. *Histoire de la philosophie.* Paris: Delagrave, 1920, 586 pp.

Giraud, Jean. *L'Eglise et les origines de la renaissance.* Paris: Lecoffre, 1902, 339 pp.

Lanson, Gustave. *Histoire de la litterature française.* Paris: Hachette, 1951, 144 pp.

Owens, Joseph. *History of Ancient Western Philosophy.* New York: Appleton, 1959, 434 pp.

Prunal, Louis. *La Renaissance catholique en France au XVIIe siècle.* Paris: Desclee, 1921, 316 pp.

68

Rayo, Antonio.	*Theology of Christian Perfection.* Dubuque: Priory Press, 1962, 692 pp.
Rivaud, Albert.	*Histoire de la philosophie.* Paris: P.U.F., 1948, 2 vol.
Villey, Pierre.	*Les Sources d'idées.* Paris: Plon, 1912, 278 pp.

2. Studies

Armstrong, Arthur.	*Christian Faith and Philosophy.* London: Darton, Longmann and Todd, 1960, 241 pp.
————————.	*An Introduction to Ancient Philosophy.* London: Methuen, 1957, 112 pp.
Bremond, Andre.	*La Piété grecque.* Paris: Bloud et Gay, 1914, 202 pp.
Bremond, Henri.	*Histoire litteraire du sentiment religieux en France depuis la fin des guerres de religion jusqu'à nos jours.* Paris: Bloud et Gay, 1929-1936, 12 vol.
————————.	*A Literary History of Religious Thought in France.* Translated by K. Montgomery. New York: MacMillan, 1936, 3 vol.
Buffenoir, Hippolyte.	*De Marc-Aurele à Napoleon.* Paris: Ambert, 1914, 350 pp.
Collot, P.	*Vraie et solide piété.* Tours: Marne, 1860, 253 pp.
Cresson, Andre.	*La Problème moral et les philosophies.* Paris: Armand Colin, 1933, 202 pp.
Dartigue-Peyrou, Jean.	*Marc-Aurele dans ses rapports avec le christianisme.* Paris: Fischvacher, 1897, 237 pp.
DeChardin, Pierre.	*The Divine Milieu.* New York: Harper, 1960, 144 pp.
Du Vair, Guillaume.	*The Moral Philosophy of the Stoics.* New Brunswick, N.J.: 1951, 134 pp.

———————————. *Traité de la constance et de la consolation.* Tolouse: La Nef, 1941, 255 pp.

Festugiere, Andre-Jean. *La Révélation d'Hermes Trismegiste.* Paris: Lecoffre, 1949, 4 vol.

———————————. *Personal Religion Among the Greeks.* London: Cambridge University Press, 1954, 179 pp.

Gore, Jeanne Lydie. *La Notion de l'indifference chez Fenelon et ses sources.* Paris: P.U.F., 316 pp.

Henriot, Emile. *XVIIe Siècle.* Paris: Editions de la Nouvelle Revue Critique, 1933, 233 pp.

Henry, A. M. *L'Initation théologique.* Paris: Cerf, 1954, 4 vol.

Hus, Alain. *Greek and Roman Religion.* New York: Hawthorn, 1962, 153 pp.

Ignace, Saint. *Exercises spirituels.* Paris: 1960, traduits et annotes par François Courd, s. j., 261 pp.

Lavelle, Louis. *The Meaning of Holiness.* New York: Pantheon, 1954, 113 pp.

Lehodey, Vital. *Le Saint abandon.* Paris: Lecoffre, 1921, 532 pp.

Louis, M. *Doctrines religieuses des philosophes grecs.* Paris: Lethielleux, 1909, 374 pp.

Mackey, Henry. *Four Essays.* London: Burns, and Oates, 1883, 96 pp.

Moeller, Charles. *Sagesse grecque et paradoxe chrétien.* Paris: Casterman, 1948, 267 pp.

Murray, Gilbert. *Stoic, Christian and Humanist.* New York: Norton, 1940, 187 pp.

Robin, Leon. *La Morale antique.* Paris: P.U.F., 173 pp.

Rodier, Georges. *Etudes de philosophie grecque.* Paris: Vrin, 354 pp.

70

Scupoli, L.	*Le Combat spirituel.* Tr. de l'italien par Morteau. Paris: Beauchesne, 1911, 241 pp.
Siguier, M.	*Antipater de Tarse et le stoicisme.* Grenoble: Merle, 1860, 125 pp.
Spannuet, Michel.	*Stoicisme des pères de l'église: de Clement de Rome à Clement d'Alexandrie.* Preface de H. I. Marrou. Paris: Seuil, 1957, 487 pp.
Werner, Charles.	*La Philosophie grecque.* Paris: Payot, 1962, 254 pp.
Zanta, Leontine.	*La Renaissance de stoicisme au XVIe siècle.* Paris: Champion, 1914, 366 pp.
Zeller, Edouard.	*Outlines of the History of Greek Philosophy.* New York: Meridian, 1960, 338 pp.

3.   *Particular Studies on Stoicism*

Aubertin, Charles.	*Seneque et Saint Paul.* Paris: Didier, 1869, 446 pp.
Bevan, Edwyn.	*Stoics and Sceptics.* Oxford: Clarendon, 1913, 152 pp.
Brehier, Emile.	*Chrysippe et l'ancien stoicisme.* Paris: P.U.F., 1951, 295 pp.
—————————.	*Les Stoiciens.* Paris: Gallimard, 1962, 1437 pp.
Brun, Jean.	*Le Stoicisme.* Paris: P.U.F., 1961, 126 pp.
Chollet, Andre.	*La Morale stoicienne en face de la morale chrétienne.* Paris: Lethielleux, 1898, 365 pp.
Dourrif, A.	*Du Stoicisme et du christianisme.* Paris: Dubuisson, 313 pp.
Favre, Jules.	*Morale des stoiciens.* Paris: Alcan, 1888, 377 pp.
Holland, Fredrick.	*The Reign of the Stoics.* New York: Somerly, 1879, 187 pp.

Hyde, William.	*The Five Great Philosophies of Life.* New York: MacMillan, 1911, 104 pp.
Pire, G.	*Stoicisme et pedagogie – de Zenon à Montaigne et à J. J. Rousseau.* Liege: Dessain, 1958, 219 pp.
Thamin, Raymond.	*Un problème moral dans l'antiquité étude sur la casuistique stoicienne.* Paris: Hachette, 1884, 350 pp.
Wenley, Robert.	*Stoicism and Its Influences.* Boston: Marshall Jones, 1924, 194 pp.

4. *Special Studies on Saint Francis de Sales*

Archambault, Paul.	*Saint François de Sales.* Paris: Lecoffre, 1930, 319 pp.
Balciunas, Vyautas.	*Vocation universelle à la perfection chrétienne selon saint François de Sales.* Rome: Université Gregorienne, 1952, 247 pp.
Calvet, Jean.	*La Litterature religieuse de François de Sales à Fenelon.* Paris: Duca, 1956, 475 pp.
Camus, Jean-Pierre.	*L'Esprit de saint François de Sales.* Riom: Thibaud-Landriot, 1835, 6 vol.
Charmot, F.	*Deux maîtres: une spiritualité – Ignace de Loyola et François de Sales.* Paris: Centurion, 1963, 318 pp.
Couannier, Maurice-Henry.	*Saint François de Sales, et ses amitiés.* Paris: Des Garets, 1922, 389 pp.
Delaruelle, Etienne.	*Saint François de Sales, maître spirituel.* Paris: Spes, 1960, 101 pp.
Hamon, M.	*Vie de saint François de Sales, évêque et prince de Geneve, docteur de l'église.* Revisée par Gonthier et Letourneau. Paris: 1922, 2 vol.
Lavaud, Benoit.	*Amour et perfection selon saint Thomas d'Aquin et saint François de Sales.*

Fribourg (Suisse): Librairie de l'Université, 1941, 341 pp.

Leclercq, Jacques.   *Saint François de Sales—docteur de la perfection.* Tournai-Paris: Casterman, 1948, 268 pp.

LeCouturier, Ernestine.   *A l'école de saint François de Sales.* Paris: Bloud et Gay, 1947, 326 pp.

Lemaire, Henry.   *François de Sales—docteur de la confiance et de la paix.* Paris: Beauchesne, 1963, 366 pp.

——————————.   *Les images chez saint François de Sales.* Paris: Nizet, 1962, 492 pp.

Liuima, Antanas.   *Aux sources du Traité de l'Amour de Dieu de saint François de Sales.* Rome: Librairie éditrice de l'Université Gregorienne, 1959, 2 vol.

Nestor, Albert.   *Somme ascetique de saint François de Sales.* Paris: Oudin, 1879, 632 pp.

Roffat, Claude.   *A L'école de saint François de Sales.* Paris: Spes, 1948, 476 pp.

——————————.   *En Retraite avec saint François de Sales.* Paris: Spes, 1954, 278 pp.

Serouet, Pierre.   *De la vie dévote à la vie mystique.* Paris: Desclee de Brouwer, 1958, 466 pp.

Strowski, Fortunat.   *Saint François de Sales.* Paris: Bloud, 1907, 364 pp.

Tessier, Henri.   *Le Sentiment de l'amour d'après saint François de Sales.* Paris: Lethielleux, 1912.

Trochu, Francis.   *Saint François de Sales—évêque et prince de Geneve.* Paris: Vitte, 1941, 2 vol.

Van Houtryve, Idesbald.   *L'Equilibre surnaturel.* Paris: Vitte, 263 pp.

——————————.   *La Vie interieure selon saint François de Sales.* Paris: Desclee de Brouwer, 1946, 254 pp.

Veuillot, Pierre.

La spiritualité salesienne de la "tressainte" indifference, thèse de theologie soutenue à l'Institut Catholique de Paris en 1947, exemplaire dactylographie, 457 pp.

Vincent, Francis.

Saint François de Sales directeur d'âmes. L'Education de la Volonté. Paris: Beauchesne, 1923, 581 pp.

5. *Articles*

Bouchardy, François.

"Saint François de Sales et le stoicisme," in *Nova et Vetera,* 4 (1934): 241-53.

Chastel, Andre.

"Art et religion dans la renaissance italienne," in *Bibliotheque d'Humanisme et Renaissance,* 7(1945): 7-40.

Des Places, Edouard.

"Religions de la Grece antique," in *l'Histoire des Religions.* Publié sous la direction de Maurice Brillant et René Aigrain. Paris: Bloud et Gay, pp. 159-292.

Jagu, Amand.

"Epictete," in *le Dictionnaire de Spiritualité.* Publié sous la direction du père André Rayez. Paris: Beauchesne, 1936, tome IV, col. 822-54.

—————————.

"Saint Paul et le stoicisme, dans la premiere moitié du XVIIe siècle. Les origines 1575-1616," in *Etudes, Franciscaines* (9 décembre 1952): 133-57, 389-410.

Pernin, R.

"Saint François de Sales," in *le Dictionnaire de Théologie Catholique.* Publié sous la direction de A. Vacant et E. Mangenot. Paris: Letouzey, 1903-1946, tome VI, col. 136-762.

Secret, Bernard.

"Saint François de Sales – Savoyard, prémier docteur de l'église de langue française," in *la Revue de Rosaire,* 8 (1960): 226-46.

Serouet, Pierre.

"Saint François de Sales," in *le Dictionnaire de Spiritualité.* Publié sous la direction du père André Rayez. Paris: Beauchesne, 1963, tome V, col. 1057-97.

Squire, Aelred.   "The Human Condition," in *Life of the Spirit*, 184 (novembre 1961): 166-82.

TORONTO STUDIES IN THEOLOGY

DATE DUE

HIGHSMITH   # 45220